JACOB'S FAMILY DRAMA

Study by Tom Allen
Commentary by Brett Younger

Free downloadable Teaching Guide for this study available at

NextSunday.com/teachingguides

NextSunday Resources
6316 Peake Road
Macon, Georgia 31210-3960
1-800-747-3016
©2019 by NextSunday Resources
All rights reserved.

TABLE OF CONTENTS

Jacob's Family Drama

Study Introduction 1

Lesson 1 Parental Favoritism
Genesis 25:21-34
　　　　Study 3
　　　　Commentary 11

Lesson 2 The Family Blessing
Genesis 27:18-41
　　　　Study 19
　　　　Commentary 27

Lesson 3 Conflict and Boundaries
Genesis 31:1-9, 17-21, 25-26, 36-42, 51-54
　　　　Study 35
　　　　Commentary 43

Lesson 4 Reconciliation
Genesis 32:3-32
　　　　Study 51
　　　　Commentary 59

Lesson 5 Closure
Genesis 33:1-17; 35:27-29
　　　　Study 67
　　　　Commentary 75

HOW TO USE THIS STUDY

NextSunday Resources Adult Bible Studies are designed to help adults study Scripture seriously within the context of the larger Christian tradition and, through that process, find their faith renewed, challenged, and strengthened. We study the Scriptures because we believe they affect our current lives in important ways. Each study contains the following three components:

Study Guide

Each study guide lesson is arranged in four movements:

Reflecting recalls a contemporary story, anecdote, example, or illustration to help us anticipate the session's relevance in our lives.

Studying is centered on giving the biblical material in-depth attention while often surrounding it with helpful insights from theology, ethics, church history, and other areas.

Understanding helps us find relevant connections between our lives and the biblical message.

What About Me? provides brief statements that help unite life issues with the meaning of the biblical text.

Commentary

Each study guide lesson is accompanied by an additional, in-depth commentary on the biblical material. Written by a different author than the study guide, each commentary gives the opportunity for learners to approach the Scripture text from a separate but complementary viewpoint.

Teaching Guide

In addition to the provided study guide and commentary, *NextSunday Resources* also provides a *free* downloadable teaching guide, available at NextSunday.com. Each teaching guide gives the teacher tools for focusing on the content of each study guide lesson through additional commentary and Bible background information. Through teacher helps and teaching options, each teaching guide also provides substance for variety and choice in the preparation of each lesson.

NextSunday
Resources

STUDY INTRODUCTION

This study follows the story of Jacob, one of the central characters of the Old Testament. Jacob was the son of Isaac and Rebekah and the grandson of Abraham and Sarah. He was also the grandson of Bethuel, father of Rebekah and Laban. Bethuel is a lesser-known figure in the Bible, but that relationship became important as the story of Jacob's life unfolded.

Jacob was later renamed Israel, "one who struggles with God and human beings." He was the ancestor of the people of Israel. Struggles of one sort or another dominated his life and that of his descendants.

In Jacob's family, God worked in the background, sometimes quietly, sometimes in direct and confrontational ways, to achieve a larger purpose. Often that purpose had a life of its own. The blessings and promises of God touched Jacob's life and the lives of his extended family, despite his clever efforts to secure those blessings and promises for himself or the efforts of others to take those blessings and promises from him.

Sometimes we idealize the people of the Bible. We forget that, like us, they were flesh-and-blood human beings. They celebrated and suffered as we do. The narratives of the Bible, honestly and compassionately drawn, lift up those people not as ideals for us to mimic or caricatures for us to despise, but as brothers and sisters and ancestors from whom we have much to learn. In them, flawed though they were, the spirit of God chose to dwell.

In this study, we focus on the relationships in Jacob's family. All of us have families. All families have strengths, weaknesses, conflicts, success stories, and unique relational patterns. The family of Isaac, Rebekah, Jacob, Esau, Leah, Rachel, and Laban is no exception. In their struggles, conflicts, and triumphs, we come to know ourselves. As they overcame, we too can overcome.

This is their story. It is our story too.

1

PARENTAL FAVORITISM

Genesis 25:21-34

Central Question

How have childhood family dynamics shaped my choices?

Scripture

Genesis 25:21-34 Isaac prayed to the LORD for his wife, because she was barren; and the LORD granted his prayer, and his wife Rebekah conceived. 22 The children struggled together within her; and she said, "If it is to be this way, why do I live?" So she went to inquire of the LORD. 23 And the LORD said to her, "Two nations are in your womb, and two peoples born of you shall be divided; the one shall be stronger than the other, the elder shall serve the younger." 24 When her time to give birth was at hand, there were twins in her womb. 25 The first came out red, all his body like a hairy mantle; so they named him Esau. 26 Afterward his brother came out, with his hand gripping Esau's heel; so he was named Jacob. Isaac was sixty years old when she bore them. 27 When the boys grew up, Esau was a skillful hunter, a man of the field, while Jacob was a quiet man, living in tents. 28 Isaac loved Esau, because he was fond of game; but Rebekah loved Jacob. 29 Once when Jacob was cooking a stew, Esau came in from the field, and he was famished. 30 Esau said to Jacob, "Let me eat some of that red stuff, for I am famished!" (Therefore he was called Edom.) 31 Jacob said, "First sell me your birthright." 32 Esau said, "I am about to die; of what use is a birthright to me?" 33 Jacob said, "Swear to me first." So he swore to him, and sold his birthright to Jacob. 34 Then Jacob gave Esau bread and lentil stew, and he ate and drank, and rose and went his way. Thus Esau despised his birthright.

Reflecting

Sarah, Sam Jr., and Steve were reared on a family farm. One by one, the siblings grew up, got married, and went off to college. When they were in their twenties, their father, Samuel, developed emphysema. Sam Jr. quit his job and returned home to help his ailing father on the farm. He discovered that he loved farm life and vowed to follow in his father's footsteps. The elder Samuel could not have been happier. The whole family seemed to support the decision.

The father had incorporated the farm as SSS Farms, Inc. Over time, he gave shares in equal number to his children. Sarah, however, soon found herself in a messy divorce and sold shares to Sam Jr. at what their father thought was a fair price. Soon Steve, too, sold shares to buy a home. Since he didn't plan to farm, everyone thought this was a wise decision.

The family got along well until the mother died unexpectedly of an aneurism. Heartbroken and still suffering from emphysema, Samuel died soon after. Suddenly, the family found itself embroiled in conflict. In particular, Sarah and Steve were bitter at Sam Jr., who now owned a majority stake in the farm. The two of them now felt that the price they had received for their shares was unfair. They insisted that they had only agreed to it so as not to upset their father.

Steve further claimed that his father had always favored Sam. Not only was Sam named for their dad, but he was outgoing and athletic, while Steve was quiet and studious. Sarah felt overlooked altogether. She too would have liked to farm, she said, but as a woman was never given the chance.

Lawsuits were filed. As legal fees mounted, Sam feared losing the farm. How had it come to this?

Studying

This lesson's Bible story is also about a rural family—Isaac and Rebekah and their twin sons, who lived in the Middle East long ago. Like many family stories, this one was passed down by word of mouth. Centuries later, someone wrote it down. As the Israelites (as we will later learn, Israel is just another name for Jacob) heard this story about their ancestors, they were better able to understand themselves. They could see themselves in it.

When a baby is born, people debate whether he looks more like his uncle or his grandmother. We may say we inherited an aunt's temper or even claim to have gotten an M.D. or a Ph.D. because our ancestors were professors of medicine many generations ago. Whether through nurture or genetics, our personalities and ways of relating to others often have a way of being passed down from generation to generation.

If we look closely, we will find a bit of ourselves, our loved ones, and perhaps even our enemies in Isaac, Rebekah, Esau, and Jacob. This is our story, too. They are our spiritual forebears, and possibly our biological kin as well.

The story begins with a problem. Isaac and Rebekah were unable to conceive a child. Many families today struggle with infertility, and some spend tens of thousands of dollars trying to have a baby. The stress can create conflict in a marriage and even a sense of competition between siblings. An adult brother without children of his own may resent the attention that his sister and her children receive from the doting grandparents. He may even unwittingly create "drama," perhaps unconsciously, to try to "win" back their attention.

Family Systems Theory, a theory of human behavior pioneered by Murray Bowen, regards problems in a family not as symptoms of a troubled individual (the "identified patient"), but as resulting from relational tensions in the family as a whole. Bowen believed healing could occur when one member could remain connected, yet avoid reacting anxiously in relationships with other family members.

In this story, Isaac prays about the problem, and Rebekah conceives. If only it were always that simple! In fact, it was not so simple. Isaac was forty when he got married (v. 20) and sixty

when he became a father (v. 26). He prayed for twenty years before God acted in the way he hoped!

The couple's joy, however, is short-lived. Rebekah has problems with the pregnancy and is afraid she will miscarry or even die. As the problems continue, she becomes increasingly depressed. "If it is to be this way, why do I live?" she says (v. 22).

There were, of course, no ultrasounds or amniocentesis tests in the ancient world. Those who faced medical difficulties often consulted a religious figure, such as a prophet or shaman. Even today, people sometimes pursue nontraditional medical approaches, especially when conventional medicine offers no answers. Hoping for answers, Rebekah consults a prophet of the Lord.

God gives her a cryptic answer: "Two nations are in your womb, and...the elder shall serve the younger." The family must have debated what this meant. Was Rebekah to have twins? If so, how could one be older than the other? When she gave birth, everyone saw that she had indeed carried twins. In fact, the second child clutched the heel of the first, as if fighting to be born first! The fraternal twins were named Esau and Jacob.

The name *Jacob* may have two meanings, both of which describe Jacob's character throughout his life. The name may mean "he takes by the heel" in line with Jacob's tendency to take advantage of others for his own self-interest. The other meaning is "he supplants"; Jacob the younger brother will supplant or take over the privileged position of his elder brother Esau by stealing his birthright and blessing. OT 35

Parents of more than one child quickly discover that each child is unique. This was especially true of Esau and Jacob. Esau loved the outdoors and became skilled as a hunter. Jacob, on the other hand, preferred to stay close to home. Like his father and grandfather, he tended livestock and crops. Raising competitive, profoundly different twins would be difficult for any parent. Sadly, parental favoritism exacerbated the differences between the children: "Isaac loved Esau...but Rebekah loved Jacob" (v. 28).

This family could undoubtedly have told many stories illustrating the twins' relationship, but one stood out. As a young man, Esau came in from a hunting expedition while Jacob toiled over a stew. Hungry and exhausted, Esau begged for the "red

stuff" his brother cooked. Esau may have thought his brother was preparing a meaty stew or even a "blood broth" that would magically revive his sagging spirit (Sarna, 182). Jacob, still "stewing" over his second-place status in his father's life, seized the opportunity. He convinced his brother to

trade his birthright for a bowl of stew. Esau agreed and even swore to it. Only when he began to eat did the elder brother discover that the "red stuff" was just lentil soup!

All his life, Jacob had tried to catch his brother by the heel. Finally, he did it. The consequences, however, haunted him all his life.

Understanding

Our theme this lesson is parental favoritism. Why do Isaac and Rebekah each feel the need to choose a favorite child? Why do they choose as they do?

One might have expected Isaac to gravitate to Jacob. Isaac too "was a quiet man, living in tents" (v. 27). But he favored Esau instead. Verse 28 says he "loved Esau because he was fond of game." Note also the role of food in 27:3-4 where Jacob steals the blessing meant for Esau. Apparently the way to Isaac's heart was indeed through his stomach!

Hendrick ter Brugghen, *Esau SellingHis Birthright,* c. 1627

But is that the whole story? Is it possible that, deep down, Isaac romanticized his son's impulsive, fly-by-the-seat-of-his-pants lifestyle? Had Isaac primarily chosen his own relatively quiet lifestyle out of deference to Abraham, his larger-than-life

father? What role did birth order play in Isaac's preference? Isaac's society granted special privileges to firstborn sons.

What of Isaac's own upbringing? He too had an older brother, a half-brother named Ishmael (16:1-16). The birth of Isaac had ultimately caused Abraham to send Ishmael and his mother far off, safely out of reach of Isaac and Sarah (21:8-21). Was this somehow a factor? Was Isaac unconsciously repeating—or reacting against—the family dynamics of the previous generation?

Rebekah, for her part, favored Jacob. Did she do this because of the prophecy about the younger son? Was he easier for her to manipulate? Or was it simply because her husband chose Esau?

What about the couple's marriage? Was it as cozy as it seems at first? Could the two have channeled their frustrations with one another into their sons? Does the twins' conflict mask unacknowledged tensions in the seemingly happily-ever-after marriage of Genesis 24?

Of course, we cannot know for certain what goes on in the inner lives of others, especially those who lived so long ago. Still, it is beneficial to ask these questions; they offer insight into ourselves.

Regardless of the ultimate reasons, the choices of Isaac, Rebekah, Esau, and Jacob set in motion dynamics that would have painful consequences for generations to come.

What About Me?

• *We find our own lives reflected in our spiritual and biological forebears.* In what ways do you find yourself following (or reacting against) patterns established by your parents or grandparents, or by mentors or friends who have influenced you?

• *We also find ourselves reflected in our descendents and others we have influenced.* In what ways do you notice your children, grandchildren, students, employees, or close friends repeating (or reacting against) your patterns of behavior, either good or bad?

• *For many reasons, we may be naturally closer to one family member than another.* With which members of your family do you feel closest? Which members take more effort to love or understand? Why?

• *Childhood relational patterns can affect us in subtle yet profound ways.* How have childhood family dynamics affected you? How have they positively or negatively shaped your relationships with your spouse, children, or friends?

• *How can we live in ways that heal the choices of our parents and ancestors?* Thich Nhat Hanh, a Vietnamese Buddhist monk, writes,

> We have to live in a way that liberates the ancestors and future generations who are inside of us. Joy, peace, freedom, and harmony are not individual matters. If we do not liberate our ancestors, we will be in bondage all our lives, and we will transmit that to our children and grandchildren. (36)

What do you think? Is this sentiment congruent with our Christian beliefs? How can Christ's Spirit in us transform the patterns and choices handed down to us by our forebears?

Resources

Walter Brueggemann, *Genesis* (Atlanta: John Knox, 1982).

Edwin H. Friedman, *Generation to Generation* (New York: Guilford, 1985).

Thich Nhat Hanh, *Touching Peace* (Berkeley CA: Palifax, 1992).

Nahum M. Sarna, *Genesis* (Philadelphia: Jewish Publication Society, 1989).

Gordan J. Wenham, *Genesis 16–50* (Dallas: Word, 1994).

PARENTAL
FAVORITISM

Genesis 25:21-34

An Irritating Frenchman

We assumed the *pommes* frites at the Eiffel Tower would taste better than the biggie fries at Wendy's because they were more expensive. A small sign read, "Minimum 15 Euros Visa." We had 20 euros left, so we decided to order our fries, hot dogs—which cost more because they did not include a bun—three drinks, and a coffee. If the total was less than 20 euros, we would use Carol's cash, and if it was more, we would use the credit card. Our order came to 21 euros, so I slid my Visa under the window. The glass was so dark I could not see the person on the other side, but a booming voice said, "You have to pay cash."

I politely replied, "Your sign says if it's more than 15 we can use Visa."

"You have to pay cash."

I calmly explained, "We don't have enough cash."

"I saw your cash."

I courteously responded, "But we only have 20, and it's 21."

"So you don't get the *café*." And he took Carol's coffee.

I graciously answered, "What? Look, we're going to use Visa to pay for what we ordered."

"You have to pay cash and no *café*."

I gently asked, "Why do you have a Visa sign if you won't take Visa?"

I helpfully suggested he take down the sign and resisted the temptation to take it down myself. As I ate my bunless wiener and shared a Sprite with my wife, I thought of clever things I wish I had said: "It's not hard to figure out why people don't like the French." "It's good you're not working for tips." "Someday you're going to appear in a Sunday school commentary."

Irritating People

Why are some people so irritating? It is an easy list to make: people who park illegally and get away with it; shoppers who stand in the middle of the escalator and will not walk up the stairs; obnoxious fans who go to your team's games, sit right behind you, and cheer for the opposing team; people like me who still write about their trip to Europe even though it was years ago.

Irritating people are exasperating, but some people go beyond irritating and become evil: narrow-minded people who do not *want* to understand anyone else's opinion; politicians who treat war as if it is inconsequential; people who say they are Christians but never do anything to help the hungry; husbands who hit their wives; liars; thieves; child molesters; drunk drivers; murderers; terrorists.

After our gourmet meal at the Eiffel Tower, our family got on a train to London. Carol, who earned an A in high school French, thought she heard that bombs had exploded. Four bombs, three in the subway and one on a bus, had blown up. At least fifty-five people were killed. What kind of people could do something so barbaric? How can any person be wicked enough to slaughter innocent people?

An Evil Hero (25:21-28)

When we come to the Bible, we want to think that the bad guys God loves are merely irritating, but they are not. They are wicked. Jacob is not mischievous. He is evil.

Like many of the births in Scripture, this story begins with a barren couple. The future father and mother pray fervently. They beg God because they understand that life is a gift. Walter Brueggemann writes, "These twins...live because prayers are answered and words are spoken. They are not given life naturally. Their destiny is shaped by the One who first spoke them into life" (*Genesis* [Atlanta: John Knox, 1986] 214).

This story is about how God surrounds bad people with good grace. The account of Jacob's life starts with what could have been the world's most interesting sonogram. The writer of Genesis wants us to know that something evil is at work in Jacob from the beginning. He is heading for trouble before he is born. His life will be difficult not only for himself, but for those around him.

Jacob fights with his brother *in the womb*. His mother knows he is trouble. Eight months into the pregnancy, she wishes she were dead. When she prays, God says, "Your children are going to be butting heads for generations." God's will is stated boldly and without justification: "the one shall be stronger than the other, the elder shall serve the younger" (25:23). The writer does not apologize for this partisanship or even seem embarrassed by it.

At birth, Jacob grabs Esau's heel. They name him Jacob, usually translated "thief" but also interpreted "heel," which suits him. Both translations foreshadow the impending conflict. Isaac, the twins' father, has good reasons for not liking Jacob. The two parents who prayed for a son quickly choose a favorite.

This description of Jacob is not a romantic stained-glass view of a biblical hero but a realistic portrait of a man created in conflict, for conflict. While his parents played a role in shaping the sibling rivalry Jacob experienced with his twin brother Esau, the writer of Genesis places the conflict at God's feet.

The Israelites must have wondered about this patriarch who was always in trouble. It seems that the author decided God was responsible for the problems.

Cheating His Brother (25:29-34)

God can make promises in spite of what people decide. This is clear in the way God overcomes the law of primogeniture. According to Deuteronomy 21:15-17, the oldest son gets twice the deal. This idea was prevalent in ancient cultures. In this story, God has other ideas.

God challenges the understanding of the younger son's lesser role. As with others who were given fewer rights—women, foreigners, and the poor—God opposes beliefs held by God's people by blessing the less favored.

Being turned away by his father was painful for a son in that male-dominated culture. Jacob's dishonesty begins with anger at Isaac and jealousy toward Esau. Jacob offers Esau food but says, "First, give me the legal rights that come with being the first-born." The text says Esau is famished. He thinks he is about to die. Jacob's manipulation is like standing on the dock with a life preserver and negotiating with a drowning man. "I'll throw you the life jacket for a hundred dollars."

The younger brother, used to dealing with disadvantages, has learned to steal what he wants. Jacob knows how to work a scam. He insists that Esau make a solemn oath. Jacob buys his hungry brother's birthright for a pot of stew.

Jacob is not merely irritating. Throughout the book of Genesis, he is portrayed as a criminal, liar, and thief. If we wrote the story, we'd have Jacob arrested. He should not get away with what he does. Granted, Esau is a few sheep short of a flock. Frederick Buechner suggests that God bypassed Esau and made Jacob heir to the great promise because it is easier to make a silk purse out of sow's ear than out of a dim bulb (*Peculiar Treasures* [New York: Harper and Row, 1979] 32).

Jacob uses his cleverness to take advantage of his own brother's desperation. Yet the writer of Genesis says Jacob is one God loves. God sees something in Jacob that no one else sees. This lying thief does not have the redeeming qualities of his grandfather Abraham, yet God loves him. Jacob steals from his family, gets away with it, and goes on to become the father of the twelve tribes of Israel. God looks at this evil person and sees one worth redeeming.

As the brothers bargain over a bowl of stew, they do not seem to understand that they are playing out the story predicted before their birth. The promise of God and the sneakiness of Jacob are not seen in tension, but as instruments working together.

Grace for the Con Artist

This story is almost unacceptable to us. We want a world where everyone gets to pick the alternatives they want. In this account, there are "some options that are closed and some choices denied" (Brueggemann, 215). Jacob had lots of possibilities, but the choices God had already made for him limited his freedom.

It seems unfair that Jacob was created with such boundaries—except for this: Do you remember Jesus' story of the shepherd looking for the lost sheep? The shepherd leaves ninety-nine good sheep to find the one that is causing trouble. Jacob is the one. King David the murderer is the one. Saint Paul, terrorist to the early Christians, is the one.

Could it be that, according to Jesus, God seeks evil people who cause horrible tragedies and offers them grace? Could there be more joy in heaven over one terrorist repenting than over ninety-nine righteous people like us? That is hard to take.

Jesus said we are supposed to love our enemies, even if they are irritating, even if they are evil. We are to be merciful even as God is merciful. Somehow Jesus is able to distinguish between hating what is evil and loving the people who do evil. Jacob exemplifies God's remarkable graciousness in the face of what would only anger us.

Grace for Evil People

Someone who steals what belongs to his feeble-minded brother can't be one of the heroes of the faith. I wish God felt exactly like I feel about people who hurt others. I want God to hate the people I hate.

Like it or not, God sees people who do horrible things differently than we do. We are supposed to imagine what leads someone to act in evil ways, to steal from his own brother, even though it is hard. We are never to excuse evil, but we need to attempt to understand.

When I learned that the bombers in London in 2005 were suicide bombers, it changed what I thought. When I learned their names, it mattered.

Sidique Khan, 30, was married and had a fourteen-month-old baby. He worked with disabled students at an elementary school. The principal said, "Sidique was great with the children and they all loved him. He did so much for them, helping them and running extra clubs and activities."

Hasib Hussain, 18, was a young man described as "charming." When he did not come home, his mother called the police. She was worried about her teenager. Shahzad Tanweer, 22, was a college graduate who majored in sports science. Shahzad's uncle said, "He had everything to live for. I can't see how he can have done this. It wasn't him. It must have been forces behind him."

One of Shahzad's friends said, "He's the kind of person who gets along with anyone. His sense of humor is very good. He's a sweet lad."

How do we reconcile these facts? Someone who kills innocent people cannot be a "sweet lad." It seems too evil to consider, but somehow these terrorists, like those of 9/11 and other incidents, thought they did what God wanted them to do. They believed it enough to blow themselves up with their victims.

Maybe it is all too terrible to understand, but what happens when we see that the perpetrators of a horrendous crime believed they did the right thing? What does it mean when you find out that your French fry salesman is going through a divorce? That the person parked illegally has a broken leg? That the sports fan feels as passionately about his team as you do about yours? That the child molester was molested as a child? That the bad parent was abused? That the drunk driver just learned that he has cancer?

In a world of indefensible wickedness, we should never excuse evil, but we should try to see more like God does, because the hard truth is that God loves people like Jacob.

Obviously, the thief has to stop stealing, the terrorist has to lay aside his or her bombs, the liar must be honest, the greedy must be generous, the powerful must be humble, the war-makers must be peacemakers, and the sinners must repent. Yet the good news does not begin with our repentance. God's love is the gospel.

The grace God offers Jacob is the same grace God offers us. It is only because God's love is unconditional that God loves you and me. God, who looks at people who do evil things and sees children worth redeeming, believes we are worth redeeming, too. Only the grace God gives to evil people is grace enough to save us.

Notes

Notes

2

THE FAMILY BLESSING

Genesis 27:18-41

Central Question

Do the members of my family know they are valued?

Scripture

Genesis 27:18-41 So he went in to his father, and said, "My father"; and he said, "Here I am; who are you, my son?" 19 Jacob said to his father, "I am Esau your firstborn. I have done as you told me; now sit up and eat of my game, so that you may bless me." 20 But Isaac said to his son, "How is it that you have found it so quickly, my son?" He answered, "Because the LORD your God granted me success." 21 Then Isaac said to Jacob, "Come near, that I may feel you, my son, to know whether you are really my son Esau or not." 22 So Jacob went up to his father Isaac, who felt him and said, "The voice is Jacob's voice, but the hands are the hands of Esau." 23 He did not recognize him, because his hands were hairy like his brother Esau's hands; so he blessed him. 24 He said, "Are you really my son Esau?" He answered, "I am." 25 Then he said, "Bring it to me, that I may eat of my son's game and bless you." So he brought it to him, and he ate; and he brought him wine, and he drank. 26 Then his father Isaac said to him, "Come near and kiss me, my son." 27 So he came near and kissed him; and he smelled the smell of his garments, and blessed him, and said, "Ah, the smell of my son is like the smell of a field that the LORD has blessed. 28 May God give you of the dew of heaven, and of the fatness of the earth, and plenty of grain and wine. 29 Let peoples serve you, and nations bow down to you. Be lord over your brothers, and may your mother's sons bow down to you. Cursed be everyone who curses you, and blessed be everyone who blesses you!" 30 As soon as Isaac had finished blessing Jacob, when Jacob had scarcely gone out from the presence of his father Isaac, his brother Esau came in from his hunting. 31 He also prepared savory food, and brought it to his father. And he said to his father, "Let my father sit up and eat of his son's game, so that you may bless me." 32 His father Isaac said to him, "Who are you?" He answered, "I am your firstborn son, Esau." 33 Then Isaac trembled violently, and said, "Who was it then that hunted game and brought it to me, and I ate it all before you came, and I have blessed him?—yes, and blessed he shall be!" 34 When Esau heard his father's words, he cried out with an exceedingly great and bitter cry, and said to his father, "Bless me, me also, father!" 35 But he said, "Your brother came deceitfully, and he has taken away your blessing." 36 Esau said, "Is he not rightly named Jacob? For he has supplanted me these two times. He took away my birthright; and look, now he has taken away my blessing." Then he said, "Have you not reserved a blessing for me?" 37 Isaac answered Esau, "I have already made him your lord, and I have given him all his brothers as servants, and with grain and wine I have sustained him. What then can I do for you, my son?" 38 Esau said to his father, "Have you only one blessing, father? Bless me, me also, father!" And Esau lifted up his voice and wept. 39 Then his father Isaac answered him: "See, away from the fatness of the earth shall your home be, and away from the dew of heaven on high. 40 By your sword you shall live, and you shall serve your brother; but when you break loose, you shall break his yoke from your neck." 41 Now Esau hated Jacob because of the blessing with which his father had blessed him, and Esau said to himself, "The days of mourning for my father are approaching; then I will kill my brother Jacob."

Reflecting

By his freshman year of high school, Freddie was already a starter in football and basketball. But he truly loved and excelled in baseball. He played catcher. When runners occasionally tried to steal second, he would hurl the ball across the diamond for an easy out. He was also an outstanding batter.

That year, on a bet, Freddie went to a Major League Baseball tryout. The scout was impressed, but knew Freddie was too young. "You snuck into this," he said, pretending to be stern. "You're supposed to be eighteen." Then he smiled. "Come back in a few years," he said. "You're good."

Freddie's father, however, was not so impressed. He scolded his son, both on and off the field, for every mistake. In addition to the varsity team at school, he enrolled Freddie in three summer leagues. Every day, the two traveled somewhere for a game or practice. Freddie stoically endured the criticism and rigorous schedule. His

> Feelings of worth can flourish only in an atmosphere where individual differences are appreciated, mistakes are tolerated, communication is open, and rules are flexible—the kind of atmosphere that is found in a nurturing family.
> —Virginia Satir

mother had left when he was a baby. He only had his father. He loved his father deeply, but however good Freddie was, it was not enough to please his dad.

Two years later, Freddie unexpectedly quit the baseball team. Soon after, he dropped out of school, moved away from home, and broke off all contact with his father. Now an adult and a heavy beer drinker, he has put on nearly 100 pounds. He looks many years older than he really is. When looking at him, one would never guess that he once seemed destined for a career in professional baseball.

Where did his life go wrong? Was it simply that his father had pushed too hard? As an adult, what responsibility does Freddie have now? How can healing take place?

Studying

The story of Jacob is the story of a man in search of his father's blessing. For whatever reason, Jacob's father, Isaac, did not seem to love him. Instead, Isaac poured his love and affection onto his other son, Jacob's twin Esau, who was older by a few minutes.

We can only guess at the reasons for this favoritism. Isaac himself grew up in a family where the father loved one son more than the other. The other, Ishmael, eventually had to leave home. Perhaps this pattern was unconsciously at work, or perhaps Isaac had in mind a certain ideal for a son. For twenty years, he and Rebekah had been unable to conceive. All that time, Isaac had prayed. He probably dreamed about what his son would be like, how he would look, what sort of relationship they would have. Perhaps little Jacob had not fit that ideal. Jacob was beautiful in his own way, but because he was not the son his father had hoped for, he was pushed away.

In this lesson's Scripture passage, Jacob and Esau are adults. Advancing in years, Isaac is blind and feeble. Esau has already married two women of pagan heritage. The Bible gives few details, except to say that his wives "made life bitter for Isaac and Rebekah" (26:35). Despite this, Isaac continues to favor Esau at the expense of Jacob. Privately, he calls for Esau and tells him to make preparations. Isaac intends to give Esau the "deathbed blessing" ahead of schedule (27:1-4).

The *blessing* in that culture was not mere money or property. The *birthright*, the theme of the last session, referred to the share of property the eldest son received from the estate. The *blessing* was different. The blessing was a spiritual power to be passed down to future generations. When fathers, late in life, spoke words of blessing over sons, the words were believed to have immense power. They were no mere wish, but self-fulfilling prophecies (see Brueggemann, 227–28).

Ordinarily, a father would bless all his sons (see Gen 48–49). In this case, however, ignoring custom, Isaac secretly plots to bless only one of his sons (Wenham, 205). But Rebekah, eavesdropping, over-hears. What went through her mind? We can imagine her saying, "Is he out of his mind?

> Blessings were also requested by and given through power-filled mediators, family heads, persists, kings, and prophets. Patriarchs blessed their heirs by both the spoken word and the laying on of hands (Gen 27:1-45; 48:1-20). In this way the tribal leader pronounced upon his people the inclusive blessing of peace (shalom), which incorporated all the positive values that make life in community meaningful. (Smith, 189)

Can he really hate us that much? Has he finally lost it?" Whatever her thoughts, she kept them to herself. Instead, always a woman of action, she went to work. If Isaac and Esau plotted to exclude Jacob, she and Jacob would plot back. If Isaac would bless only one son, he would bless *her* favorite son, her Jacob!

She decided to turn Jacob into Esau, but they needed to hurry. Isaac asked Esau to kill fresh game. That would take time. But Esau was a skilled hunter. Who knew how long they had?

Old Isaac could not see, but his other senses were fine. Isaac had asked Esau to prepare his favorite dish. Rebekah knew she could fix one just like it. She could also dress Jacob in his brother's clothes. But what about his skin? Esau was hairy, but Jacob was smooth. She put lambskins on his hands and neck. As for Isaac's hearing, Jacob would have to give his best Esau impersonation. Would it work? Jacob was unsure (27:11-12), but ultimately committed himself to the ruse.

From the moment Jacob entered the room, Isaac doubted. His son arrived too soon. Esau was a good hunter, but not *that* good! Isaac also doubted the voice. Jacob talked too much and almost gave himself away (Wenham, 208). But the skins on his hands and neck and the dish his mother prepared were convincing. Isaac, now with a full stomach and also full of wine (v. 25), blessed his son.

Esau returned soon after, dish in hand, to claim his blessing. When father and son discovered what had happened, they were aghast. The blessing had a power all its own. Once he issued it, Isaac could not recall it. Isaac "trembled violently." Esau, the tough man of the open country, sobbed pitifully. "Bless me, me also, father!" he cried (v. 38). But little blessing remained. Isaac,

> The Hebrew language of Isaac's blessing for Esau in verses 39-40 is vague. It could mean that Esau will dwell "away from" the bounty of the land or that he too will also experience God's blessing. Perhaps Isaac is carefully trying to edit his terrible mistake through words that can have a double meaning. (Sarna, 194)
>
> Also, the blessing definitely ends on a positive note, insisting that in spite of the troubles ahead, ultimately the children of Esau will also experience freedom. "In the midst of Jacob's coup, liberation for other peoples is also envisioned" (Brueggemann, 234).

intending it all for Esau, unwittingly gave it all to Jacob. Their plan backfired horribly.

The scene ends with Esau fuming, seeking an opportunity to kill his brother. It would be a hard road ahead.

Understanding

Why did Isaac find it so difficult to love Jacob? Whatever the reasons, Jacob spent his whole life grasping for the blessing his father never willingly gave. Years later, the Bible tells how "a man" accosted Jacob at a riverbank. Wrestling until dawn, the stranger finally conceded that the fight was a stalemate and asked Jacob to let him go. "I will not let you go unless you bless me," said Jacob (Gen 32:26). Poor Jacob was so desperate for a blessing that he sought one even from a violent stranger!

Many people are like this. Perhaps our father or mother was unable to show us that we were loved and valued when we were young. Why? Maybe our parents themselves did not experience love and appreciation as children. Maybe we did not conform to their ideals of what a son or daughter should be like. Perhaps they suffered from mental illness, addiction, abuse, abandonment, or the traumas of war or life.

> Have you ever been desperate for the approval of someone important to you?

If we cannot recognize our own situation for what it is and come to terms with it, we may spend our whole lives searching desperately for the blessing we never received from our parents. We may search for it in overwork, in alcohol or other drugs, or in the arms of a stranger or violent lover. Moreover, we may unwittingly fail to bless one or more of our own children, transmitting the curse to future generations.

Sadly, Jacob was unable to break the cycle. In later years, he repeated the pattern of his parents and grandparents, favoring one son, Joseph, at the expense of the others. This caused all of them considerable suffering. It was left to righteous Joseph to try to break the cycle.

What About Me?

• *Words and symbolic actions are not to be taken for granted.* When transmitted with authority, they have considerable power. How does it affect a child if a parent tells her she will "never amount to anything," or that he will "wind up in prison"? Can a child shrug it off if a teacher tells her she has no aptitude in math? If little girls only see males speaking or leading in church, what unspoken message does this send?

• *It is important that we come to terms with how the words and actions of others have shaped our lives.* Can you remember a time when parents or teachers suggested, by their words or silence, that you were not valued or were valued less than others? How has that experience influenced you? How did your parents and others bless and encourage you? How did they convey these blessings? How have those experiences influenced you?

• *We need to choose with great care the words we speak over others.* Have you said something to someone, perhaps out of anger, that you now regret? How can you repair the damage of your words? How are you seeking to bless your own children, students, or others God has placed in your life? What words or symbolic gestures can you give them that will let them know they are loved?

• *The grace of God can transform the curses we receive from others.* Jacob was unable to break the pattern of his family. But in the next generation, Joseph spoke of how his brothers intended harm, but God "intended it for good" (50:20) (cf. Ps 109:28; Matt 5:11). In what ways can God transform our childhood "baggage" so we can bless others?

Resources

Walter Brueggemann, *Genesis* (Atlanta: John Knox, 1982).

Edwin H. Friedman, *Generation to Generation* (New York: Guilford, 1985).

Myron C. Madden, *The Power to Bless* (Nashville: Abington, 1970).

Nahum M. Sarna, *Genesis* (Philadelphia: Jewish Publication Society, 1989).

David A. Smith, "Curse and Blessing," *Mercer Dictionary of the Bible*, ed. Watson E. Mills et al. (Macon GA: Mercer University Press, 1990).

Gordan J. Wenham, *Genesis 16–50* (Dallas, Texas: Word, 1994).

THE FAMILY
BLESSING
Genesis 27:18-41

The Players

The 1973 classic movie *The Sting* starred Paul Newman and
Robert Redford as lovable con artists. They were so charming
that the audience almost forgot they were thieves. Viewers adored
them even though you would not want to stand next to them in
line at the bank. The film included chapter headings describing
the divisions in the story such as "The Players," "The Set-Up,"
"The Tale," "The Shut-Out," and "The Sting."

In our Bible story, Jacob is also a lovable con artist. He could
be so charming that his victims almost forgot he was a thief. He
was adored even though no one would want him near their
birthright or blessing.

We can only speculate whether Jacob desired his father's
blessing to compensate for feelings of rejection. His actions drove
a deeper wedge between him and the rest of his family. We do not
always recognize the mystical nature of the bond between fathers
and children, but the writer of Genesis understood. The approval
or disapproval of a father often seems to make or break a child's
life. We long to be blessed.

The ancient ideas seem foreign, but we should take the act of
blessing more seriously. For the players in this story, the blessing
is more important than what meets the eye. Blessing acknowledges
the power of a spoken word and the hope of a high calling.

Genesis 27 is the sequel to the story of the birthright
(25:19-34). The two stories depict the way the promise passed
from one generation to the next. Our attention is drawn to the
sibling rivalry, but the bigger picture is how people live out God's

decree. The promise goes to Jacob the younger instead of Esau the elder. The blessing of God seems to have a life of its own.

The Set-Up

The old man must give his blessing before he dies (27:4). For Isaac, the act of blessing is the bestowing of genuine power. We often think of words as fleeting, but the words of blessing shape the recipient's life. Isaac, Esau, Rebekah, and Jacob believe the blessing, not money and power, will determine the future. They understand that someone is going to be left out. Jacob wants the patriarchal blessing, and he and his mother are willing to deceive his father to get it. Jacob is trying to correct the order of his birth.

While Rebekah eavesdrops, Isaac explains to Esau how he will give him the blessing. Rebekah believes she should take the blessing for Jacob, so she carefully plans the con.

Rebekah dresses Jacob in Esau's clothes, supplying goatskin gloves and an extra pelt to wrap around his neck. Her plan is clearly dishonest. To someone who does not read the Bible often, this kind of story may not seem like it belongs.

The Tale

Jacob is about forty years old when he decides to trick Isaac, who is almost blind and shows signs of dementia, into thinking he is Esau and giving him the blessing. Jacob hopes he can perform well enough to pull off his mother's plan.

"Father," he says.

Isaac asks, "Which son are you?"

Jacob takes a deep breath and begins the tall tale. "It's Esau, your firstborn. I did what you asked. I made the game you ordered and will wait for your blessing."

Isaac is not sure what to think. "How did you do it so quickly?"

Jacob, who keeps sinking lower and lower, answers, "God was on my side helping me."

Isaac is still not certain. "Let me touch you, just to be sure."

Jacob moves forward and puts out his hand. Now Isaac is even more confused. "You feel like Esau, but you sound like Jacob."

Despite his bewilderment, he finally says, "Okay. Dish it out. Let's do this."

Jacob finishes setting the table and brings a big jug of wine.

After eating, Isaac pushes his plate away and says, "Give me a hug and a kiss."

Jacob kisses him, and Isaac catches a whiff of Esau's clothes. Isaac cannot trust his hearing, and his bad circulation makes it hard to be sure of what he touches, but his nose still works. The familiar aroma convinces him. Isaac gives out a blessing to end all blessings: "The smell of my son is like the smell of God's great outdoors. I give you this blessing. May God give you dew in the morning and harvests of grain and wine. May others serve you and nations honor you. You will be over your brothers, your mother's sons. Those who curse you will regret it. Those who are kind to you will be blessed."

The Shut-Out

Just as Jacob slips out the door, Esau walks in. He has prepared a great meal. "Father," he says, "dinner's ready. Come and eat what I have cooked so that you may give me your blessing."

Confused, Isaac wonders, "Who are you?"

"It's me, Esau. Who else could it be?"

Isaac starts shaking. "Then who was just here? Who killed the game and made the meal and served it to me and received my blessing? Whom did I bless forever?"

Esau begins to sob. "Father, you have to bless me. You can't completely shut me out. You must have some blessing left for me, too."

Isaac realizes what has happened and can only agree with Esau about how horrible it is. "Your brother tricked me. He has your blessing."

Esau says, "You got the heel's name right. The thief has stolen from me twice—first my birthright and now my blessing. You have to have something left for me."

Isaac answers, "I gave him everything. I promised him power over you and all his brothers, grain, and wine. There's nothing left to give you." (This is a somewhat curious promise as Genesis has not mentioned any other brothers.)

Esau weeps bitterly. "There has to be something left for me. Anything. Please. I beg you."

The blessing Esau receives is not what he wants. Isaac mournfully says, "Your life will be hard. You will have to fight and work for every little thing you get. You brother will always win. The best day for you will be when you get away from your brother for good."

Twice Jacob has cheated his lame-brained brother out of what is rightfully his. How would you respond if your twin brother went to your senile father on his deathbed, lied to him, and had you written out of the will? Esau is furious. He decides to kill his brother. "The day my father dies is the day my brother dies," he vows. A jury would have given Esau probation.

Rebekah has to get Jacob out of town in a hurry. He makes his getaway into the hill country to the north (27:43). It is ironic that the blessing makes Jacob a fugitive. The blessing, intended for good, tears the family apart. If Rebekah ever saw Jacob again, it is not recorded.

The Sting

While it is true that Jacob and Rebekah pulled off quite a sting operation to steal the blessing, it is also true that the writer of Genesis seems to believe that dishonesty is a tool by which the blessing moves as God intended. Rebekah is more than a manipulative mother. There is something other than mere favoritism at work. Maybe she is willing to risk a curse (27:13) because she feels responsible for what she heard God say (25:23). John Claypool argued that Rebekah had as much to do with keeping the traditions of Abraham alive as anyone (*Glad Reunion* [Waco: Word, 1985] 21–29).

Rebekah plays her part because Isaac does not. To understand Rebekah's position in the family, we need to remember what happened to her husband before she arrived.

As a boy, Isaac experienced something that surely marked him for life. Somehow, Abraham became convinced that he was to take Isaac, his long-awaited son, and sacrifice him to God (22:9-14). It must have scarred this twelve-year-old to be laid on top of a woodpile, watching as his father raised a knife over his head. For the rest of his days, Isaac kept his distance from his father's God. He did not rebel completely, but neither did he ever venture near to the One with whom Abraham seemed so close. God's promises do not seem overly important to Isaac, and that is the reason Rebekah is so important.

She kept the promises to Abraham alive. Like most of the people of that day, Abraham was serious about family purity. When the time came, he sent a servant back to the members of his family in Mesopotamia to secure a wife for Isaac. This is a peculiar love story. The servant first encounters Rebekah at the great gathering place of ancient culture, the community well. Rebekah is described as "fair to look upon" (24:16). She draws water not only for the servant, but also for his camels. He is quick to begin negotiating with Rebekah's family for her to become Isaac's wife.

Perhaps this servant's stories were Rebekah and her family's first encounter with the mysterious promises God made to Abraham and his descendants. Rebekah left on a journey that was every bit as daring as Abraham's was several decades earlier (Claypool, 24). She set out with a stranger to marry a man she had never seen. The burden of keeping alive the sacred stories became Rebekah's.

Isaac and Rebekah had an unusually intimate marriage for that time. The old *Book of Common Prayer* includes these words in the marriage ceremony: "As Isaac and Rebekah lived faithfully together, so may these persons surely perform the vows and covenants betwixt them made."

When, after years of barrenness, Rebekah finally became pregnant, she felt joy and relief, followed by excruciating pain. She asked God what was happening, and God let her in on the secret, as we studied last session: "Two nations are in your womb, and two peoples born of you shall be divided; the one shall be stronger than the other, the elder shall serve the younger" (25:23).

Rebekah never forgot that word from God, which explains many of her actions that at first appear to be little more than personal preference of one son over the other.

If you read Genesis in light of the prophecy Rebekah heard, it appears that she is not merely playing favorites with the child she likes best. The word God gave Rebekah became the focus of her life. God's word was that Esau should serve Jacob. Rebekah obeyed that vision even though it cost her dearly. When she overheard Isaac tell Esau that it was time to pass on the blessing, she immediately worked to get what God said should go to Jacob. Rebekah took God's intentions more seriously than Isaac did. What Rebekah did for Jacob is deceptive, but in light of the larger good—keeping alive the promises made to Abraham—her actions seem heroic.

Russian theologian Nicolas Berdyaev has noted the difference between what he calls "the ethics of obedience" and "the ethics of creativity." The ethics of obedience refers to following the rules, while the ethics of creativity points to exceptional moments when people are called to violate lesser laws in the name of a higher law. What Dietrich Bonhoeffer did in participating in the plot on Hitler's life and what Martin Luther King Jr. did in his acts of civil disobedience are examples of the ethics of creativity. Rebekah's actions, too, seem like an ethics of creativity that kept the covenant alive (Claypool, 26–27).

Rebekah is numbered in the sacred company of those who obey God above all others. The stories of Abraham might have been lost without her sacrifice. We have to choose whether we will center our lives on God's promises. The God of Rebekah empowers us to be courageous and faithful.

Notes

Notes

3

CONFLICT
AND BOUNDARIES

Genesis 31:1-9, 17-21, 25-26, 36-42, 51-54

Central Question

What lines must I draw for my own well-being and that of my family?

Scripture

Genesis 31:1-9, 17-21, 25-26, 36-42, 51-54 Now Jacob heard that the sons of Laban were saying, "Jacob has taken all that was our father's; he has gained all this wealth from what belonged to our father." 2 And Jacob saw that Laban did not regard him as favorably as he did before. 3 Then the LORD said to Jacob, "Return to the land of your ancestors and to your kindred, and I will be with you." 4 So Jacob sent and called Rachel and Leah into the field where his flock was, 5 and said to them, "I see that your father does not regard me as favorably as he did before. But the God of my father has been with me. 6 You know that I have served your father with all my strength; 7 yet your father has cheated me and changed my wages ten times, but God did not permit him to harm me. 8 If he said, 'The speckled shall be your wages,' then all the flock bore speckled; and if he said, 'The striped shall be your wages,' then all the flock bore striped. 9 Thus God has taken away the livestock of your father, and given them to me...." 17 So Jacob arose, and set his children and his wives on camels; 18 and he drove away all his livestock, all the property that he had gained, the livestock in his possession that he had acquired in Paddan-aram, to go to his father Isaac in the land of Canaan. 19 Now Laban had gone to shear his sheep, and

Rachel stole her father's household gods. 20 And Jacob deceived Laban the Aramean, in that he did not tell him that he intended to flee. 21 So he fled with all that he had; starting out he crossed the Euphrates, and set his face toward the hill country of Gilead.... 25 Laban overtook Jacob. Now Jacob had pitched his tent in the hill country, and Laban with his kinsfolk camped in the hill country of Gilead. 26 Laban said to Jacob, "What have you done? You have deceived me, and carried away my daughters like captives of the sword...." 36 Then Jacob became angry, and upbraided Laban. Jacob said to Laban, "What is my offense? What is my sin, that you have hotly pursued me? 37 Although you have felt about through all my goods, what have you found of all your household goods? Set it here before my kinsfolk and your kinsfolk, so that they may decide between us two. 38 These twenty years I have been with you; your ewes and your female goats have not miscarried, and I have not eaten the rams of your flocks. 39 That which was torn by wild beasts I did not bring to you; I bore the loss of it myself; of my hand you required it, whether stolen by day or stolen by night. 40 It was like this with me: by day the heat consumed me, and the cold by night, and my sleep fled from my eyes. 41 These twenty years I have been in your house; I served you fourteen years for your two daughters, and six years for your flock, and you have changed my wages ten times. 42 If the God of my father, the God of Abraham and the Fear of Isaac, had not been on my side, surely now you would have sent me away empty-handed. God saw my affliction and the labor of my hands, and rebuked you last night." ... 51 Then Laban said to Jacob, "See this heap and see the pillar, which I have set between you and me. 52 This heap is a witness, and the pillar is a witness, that I will not pass beyond this heap to you, and you will not pass beyond this heap and this pillar to me, for harm. 53 May the God of Abraham and the God of Nahor"—the God of their father—"judge between us." So Jacob swore by the Fear of his father Isaac, 54 and Jacob offered a sacrifice on the height and called his kinsfolk to eat bread; and they ate bread and tarried all night in the hill country.

Reflecting

Art and Sarah have two adult children. Their son Doug lost his job and went through a painful divorce soon afterward. He asked his parents if he could move back home. What could they do? He was still their son. They welcomed him home, asking few questions about his marriage or employment. They did not think it was their place to pry into his personal affairs.

Then they noticed that Doug seemed somewhat depressed. He was not motivated to find a new job. Mostly, he stayed in his old room, spending time on the computer. At night he went out with friends, often not returning until early morning. He also frequently asked his parents for money. When they occasionally said no, he sulked like a small child.

Art and Sarah became increasingly concerned. Was Doug clinically depressed? Was he taking drugs, perhaps prescription painkillers? What was he doing on the Internet for hours and when he went out at night?

Art felt that it was time to confront Doug about these issues. Sarah disagreed. "He is our son," she said. "We must love him unconditionally." The situation drove all three of them apart. They lived in the same household, but they rarely spoke or interacted with one another. Doug's physical presence, compounded with his emotional absence, was tearing the family apart.

What counsel would you give to this family? For all their good intentions, were Art and Sarah really helping their son? Are there appropriate boundaries they should set with him? What steps can this family take toward a better life, together or separately?

Studying

Last lesson's passage ended with Jacob and Rebekah tricking Isaac into blessing Jacob instead of his twin brother, Esau. In this lesson's passage, twenty years have passed, and it is helpful to review those intervening years.

Esau, enraged that Jacob had acquired his birthright and blessing, plotted to kill his brother. Rebekah discovered the plot and devised plans of her own. On the pretext that Jacob should marry within the clan, she arranged to send him off to live with her family in Aram. She intended for him to stay only "a while" (27:44). Sadly, she never saw him again.

Jacob found his way to the home of Laban, his mother's brother, who received him joyfully. Jacob also met his beautiful cousin Rachel, and a month later, arrangements were made for him to marry her. Ordinarily, a "bride price" was required, which the woman's family held for her in trust. In this case, since Jacob was penniless, Laban arranged for Jacob to work for him for seven years instead.

> While *monogamy* (one man, one woman) was the ideal for marriage (Gen 3:24), *polygamy*, the practice of having more than one spouse, was also common in the ancient world. In particular, wealthy or powerful men often had more than one wife or concubine (ch. 16; 25:1-2).
>
> *Endogamy*, the custom of marrying within one's tribe or clan, was also common. For example, Abraham married his half-sister Sarah (Gen 20:12), Nahor married his niece Milcah (11:29), Isaac married his cousin Rebekah (24:15), Esau married his cousin Mahalath (28:9), and Jacob married his cousins Rachel and Leah (29:12) (Hamilton, 4:563–65).

The years passed, and the wedding took place. The next morning, Jacob expected to find beautiful Rachel by his side. Instead, he found Leah, Rachel's older sister (29:25)! When Jacob complained that this was not the bargain, Laban claimed it was local custom for the firstborn daughter to marry first. Moreover, Jacob could still marry Rachel too, provided he agreed to seven more years of servitude. In Laban, Jacob had met his match. His uncle was as much a conman as Jacob was!

During the next seven years, Jacob fathered eleven sons and a daughter by his two wives and two concubines. (A twelfth son was born later.) Having completed his terms of service, Jacob asked to return home, but Laban would not let him go so easily. Laban saw an opportunity to enrich himself through Jacob and his eleven boys.

Always a smooth talker, Laban convinced Jacob to stay on as an employee, with a portion of the livestock as his wages. A battle of wits followed, with Jacob using selective breeding (and a little superstition) to increase his share of the livestock, while Laban constantly tried to get the best of Jacob. In the end, neither man's scheming amounted to much. The Lord was with Jacob. In those

six years, Jacob "grew exceedingly rich, and had large flocks, and male and female slaves, and camels and donkeys" (30:43). But Jacob's success also brought conflict with Laban's sons (31:1-2).

At this point, we pick up this lesson's passage. God tells Jacob to return to his homeland (31:3), but it is not easy. When Jacob had first fled, he had traveled alone. Now a large family, servants, and livestock must go with him. There was also the matter of Laban, who had detained him for many years (29:27; 30:25-28) and even now could simply refuse to let them go (31:31).

Jacob's first action is to meet privately with his wives to secure their support. His relationships with Leah and Rachel were not without conflict (29:31; 30:1-2). Still, he makes his case, recounting the past years and emphasizing God's providential care (31:5). Persuaded, they offer their support for their husband against their father (31:14-16).

Jacob chooses Laban's busiest time of year—when sheep are sheared—to make his escape. His caravan gets a head start, but Laban soon catches up (31:25). God warns Laban not to use force (31:24, 29), so the two battle with words. Laban accuses Jacob of kidnapping at worst and incivility at best. He should have at least been allowed to kiss his daughters goodbye, he says (31:28). More serious is the matter of Laban's household gods, which he accuses Jacob of stealing.

When a search for the missing gods (which Rachel had taken) produces no evidence, it is Jacob's turn to vent (31:36-42). Laban is still angry, but there is little he can do (31:43). Finally, he asks Jacob for a formal covenant of separation. If they are to part, they will do so as equals. The two households enter into covenant along with a sacrificial meal, as is customary, and erect a monument for future generations. Having agreed to part peaceably, the families go their separate ways (31:55).

The *household gods* were idols that were believed to carry with them power, prosperity, and the legal claim to the family's property. OT 44

Understanding

Conflict can occur even in the best of families. Jacob left his family and homeland to avoid conflict with his brother Esau. But in Aram, with the family of his mother, he encountered conflict of a different nature. In his uncle Laban, Jacob found a trickster as devious as himself. Eventually, their conflict escalated to the point that Jacob had to move away with his wives and children. He and Laban established boundaries so that each side of the family could move forward. The two men parted, if not amicably, then at least with the awareness that they could not continue as before.

Sometimes it is necessary to take similar steps in our families. A spouse may find it necessary to pursue separation or divorce because of infidelity, abuse, or neglect. Sometimes a family member may find it necessary to put in place firm boundaries so as not to further enable a child, parent, sibling, or other loved one to continue self-destructive behaviors. Occasionally, loving parents may have to insist that their children have no contact with a particular family member—for example, if there are concerns about sexual or physical abuse. There are also occasions when, out of love, we may have to involve the authorities in an effort to get necessary psychiatric care for a family member.

Life is often difficult. While the story of Jacob and Laban is beautiful storytelling, it is not merely an account of two families in the ancient world. In these flawed but beautiful people, we also see ourselves.

Are there healthy boundaries to draw during times of conflict? How do we do this in a way that honors God and one another?

Are you more likely to stay out of a family conflict, hoping it will eventually blow over, or to enter the fray despite the risks to your relationships? How do we decide which approach is preferable in a given situation?

What About Me?

• *We need to be honest as we assess our relationships.* Jacob recognized that his father-in-law had been dishonest—not only in their business relationship, but also in the matter of Jacob's marriage to

Rachel and Leah. Has someone you loved and trusted ever cheated you?

• *In our conflicts with others, we come to know ourselves better.* In Laban, Jacob found a mirror of himself. Just as Laban cheated Jacob, Jacob had cheated Esau. Laban, Rebekah, and Jacob were very much alike. Often the flaws in others that trouble us most are the flaws we find also in ourselves. Reflect on a personal conflict. Do you find yourself reflected in some way in your adversary? Do you share some of the same flaws, though perhaps to a lesser degree?

• *In times of conflict, it is helpful to plan our response carefully and seek support from others.* Do you agree with Jacob's decision to leave without first discussing the situation with his uncle? Can you think of situations where it may be necessary to put distance between yourself and a family member without first talking about your issues? Before leaving, Jacob discussed the situation with Leah and Rachel. In a conflict, to whom would you turn for advice and support?

• *It is necessary to establish clear boundaries so that both sides can move forward.* Eventually, Jacob and Laban expressed their differences face to face. Though they were unable to reconcile, they nonetheless "agreed to disagree" and to part peaceably. How can we find a way to part peaceably from someone who has made our lives miserable?

Resources

Walter Brueggemann, *Genesis* (Atlanta: John Knox, 1982).

Henry Cloud and John Townsend, *Safe People* (Grand Rapids: Zondervan, 1995).

Edwin H. Friedman, *Generation to Generation* (New York: Guilford, 1985).

Victor P. Hamilton, "Marriage (Old Testament and Ancient Near East)," *The Anchor Bible Dictionary* (New York: Doubleday, 1992).

Nahum M. Sarna, *Genesis* (Philadelphia: Jewish Publication Society, 1989).

Gordan J. Wenham, *Genesis 16–50* (Dallas: Word, 1994).

CONFLICT
AND BOUNDARIES

Genesis 31:1-9, 17-21, 25-26, 36-42, 51-54

Con Artists

Paul Rebbins, an unknown artist, visited the New York Museum of Art. As he looked around, he began to think that his paintings were as good as some of those on display. He also realized how unlikely it was that one of his paintings would ever hang in the New York Museum of Art. The next day, he quietly brought in a painting and carefully hung it on an empty wall. He placed a plaque underneath that read, "This painting is on loan from the private collection of Donald Trump." Then he sat on a bench nearby to listen to people comment on his painting. Most were complimentary. Several days passed before anyone suspected that his painting did not belong. When museum officials realized what he had done, they removed the painting, but word got out that Paul Rebbins had a painting on display at the New York Museum of Art. Today, his paintings sell for far more than before because a clever artist put together an empty wall and his weariness with being overlooked. How many scores of artists have walked through the museum and thought their paintings good enough to be there, but never thought to hang one on the wall? One sneaky painter knew how to think outside the box.

God's people are not always known for this kind of creativity. Church folks tend to avoid risks. We get used to doing only what we are used to doing. We are timid. Identifying what made God choose Jacob is difficult, but maybe part of it was Jacob's willingness to take chances and act surprisingly.

Jacob Prepares to Leave (31:1-16)

In his father-in-law, Laban, Jacob finds a trickster as devious as himself. Laban's sons complain that Jacob has stolen from their father. Jacob realizes what is happening. Laban has "had it up to here" with his son-in-law.

Jacob hears God say, "It's time for you to go home." God's instructions to Jacob to leave Haran sound like God's command to Abraham to leave the same area (12:1-3).

Jacob sends for his wives—Laban's daughters—Rachel and Leah. They meet in the field so no one will overhear them. Jacob is not sure his wives will leave their father's house. Rachel and Leah have never lived anywhere else. The fact that Jacob discusses this with his wives rather than simply telling them they are going to Canaan indicates that daughters customarily asked their father's permission before leaving (John Hartley, *Genesis* [Peabody MA: Hendrickson, 2000] 271).

Jacob points out that while their father has not been good to them, the God of Jacob's father has. "Your father is not happy with me," he says. "He has cheated me ten times. [Ten is a round number indicating many.] He promised things he didn't deliver, but God keeps making sure I win. When your dad said, 'You can have all the speckled ones,' suddenly all the baby goats were speckled. When your dad said, 'Let's switch so you get the streaked ones,' the newborns were all streaked."

Archaeologists have found ancient contracts between owners and shepherds that were negotiated annually. Laban is trying to get terms that will increase his percentage of the flocks, but God keeps blessing Jacob. These two con men struggle to outsmart one another.

God shows Jacob in a dream how to breed goats so that the number in his flock will multiply. The angel in the dream assures Jacob that the great increase in his flock is compensation for the way Laban treats him.

Jacob's wives feel like their father has mistreated them, too. Since these two sibling rivals seldom agree, it seems likely that Laban has in fact treated them poorly. They say, "God is taking for you what belonged to us in the first place. If God is telling you to go home, we'll start packing."

Jacob Makes a Break for It (31:17-24)

Jacob decides to sneak off while Laban is away shearing sheep—a task that takes several days. Jacob loads up the camels and steals away, heading back to Isaac with lots of livestock. Laban is left totally unaware.

Cecil B. DeMille should have filmed this scene. Do you remember the exodus in the 1956 version of *The Ten Commandments*—argumentative donkeys, ramshackle carts, confused goats, sleeping children, and children the travelers wish were sleeping? Imagine that scene with Jacob at the front telling everyone, "Shush. We don't want Laban to hear us."

From Laban's point of view, Jacob has double-crossed him, conning him out of most of his livestock. When Laban looks the other way, Jacob slips off with not only the man's daughters, but just about anything else that is not nailed down.

Jacob does not know that Rachel has stolen her father's small household idols. These gods were thought to bring good fortune, fertility, and protection during a journey. Perhaps Rachel took them as partial compensation for the losses she suffered from Laban or because she wanted some tie to her family.

Jacob and his crowd are across the river and three days down the road before Laban realizes the rascal has made off with almost everything. Laban gathers a posse and goes after Jacob.

God continues to protect the heir of the promise, coming to Laban in a dream and saying, "Be careful what you do to Jacob."

Laban Catches Jacob (31:25-42)

Laban's gang does not have to stop nearly so often for bathroom breaks, so he catches Jacob in a week. The hill country of Gilead is close to 400 miles away—a journey of more than seven days for shepherds driving herds. This has led some scholars to think seven is a symbolic number.

Laban tries to sound like a heartbroken father: "What are you thinking? How could you sneak off? You kidnapped my daughters. You didn't even let me throw them a going-away party. You ought to be ashamed of yourself. Shouldn't I get to say goodbye? You wouldn't even let me kiss my daughters and grandchildren. This was a stupid thing for you to do. I could punish you for what you've done, but your God is still looking out for you and told me not to do anything to you."

Laban assumes that God's limitations do not keep him from receiving compensation for outright theft. Laban is more intent on recovering his gods than his daughters. He values symbols of his family more than his family.

"I could understand if you had said, 'I need to go home,' but that doesn't explain why you stole my gods," he continues.

Jacob admits that he has violated custom, but Laban's pattern of behavior makes it clear that he would not have bid his daughters a cheerful goodbye. "What did you expect?" Jacob asks. "I assumed you would take my wives away." Jacob still does not know what Rachel has done, so he continues, "But if anyone on my side took your gods, they should die for it. If you can find any of your stuff, it's yours to take."

Laban goes through Jacob's tent, Leah's tent, and the tents of the two maids, but finds nothing. Rachel has placed the household gods inside the camel cushion on which she sits. When Laban goes through her tent, searching high and low without finding a thing, Rachel politely informs her father that she cannot stand because she is having her period.

Ancient Israelites would have understood that the writer is poking fun at these idols. They believed anything that came in contact with a woman during her period was contaminated (Lev 15:10-23).

Now it is Jacob's turn to get irate. "Laban, what do you have to be angry about? You have ransacked everything I own. Have you turned up a single thing that's yours? Let's see it. Display the evidence. Our two families can be the jury and decide between us."

Jacob tries to exonerate himself. He recounts how hard Laban has worked him and how well Laban has done. Because of Jacob's skillful shepherding, the sheep never miscarried. When wild beasts tore apart any member of the flock, Jacob took the loss, even though standard practice did not hold a shepherd accountable for losses beyond his control (Exod 22:9-13). Shepherds were financially responsible for thefts that took place during the day, but not at night. Laban, however, demanded payment for every lost sheep. Jacob was out in all kinds of weather, from torrid heat to freezing cold, putting in many a sleepless night.

"Twenty years I have slaved for you," he tells his father-in-law, "fourteen years for your daughters, six years for a flock, and you changed my wages ten times. If you had your way, I would have left penniless, but the God of my grandfather and the Fear of my father has been watching out for me."

Laban and Jacob Agree to a Truce (31:43-55)

Laban is still patronizing, refusing to admit Jacob's role in increasing the flocks. Laban argues that it all belongs to him, but he knows he has lost. He could not prove that Jacob stole his gods, and Jacob has given a strong defense for sneaking off. In an attempt to save face, Laban calls for a truce.

Laban wants a boundary between his people and Jacob's because he has begun to fear Jacob. Jacob tells his crowd to make a pile of stones and then have a picnic beside it. The details are confusing—two witnesses, two place names, two meals, two names for God. This may indicate two sources for the story, but it could also be a rhetorical tool to emphasize the importance of the events. Each party names the pile of stones in his own language. Laban labels it in Aramaic, *Yegar-sahadutha* ("witness monument"). Jacob echoes the naming in Hebrew, *Galeed* ("witness monument").

While Laban's statement, "The LORD watch between you and me, when we are absent one from the other," looks great on a Hallmark card, in Genesis it is not a promise of friendship but a call for God to act as judge if Jacob abuses Laban's daughters or takes other wives. Prohibitions against mistreating daughters are frequently found in marriage contracts in the ancient Near East.

The word "harm" (31:52) is suggestive. Technically it was possible that someone from Jacob's family could return to Haran with the family gods and make a claim against Laban's own household (Hartley, 277). This pact ended the practice of Abraham's offspring returning to Haran to take wives.

If fences make good neighbors, then maybe boundaries make good family. Each side can move forward. The two men part, if not amicably, then at least with the awareness that they cannot continue to fight.

Laban indicates his belief in more than one god when he says, "the God of Abraham and the God [god?] of Nahor." Jacob swears only by the Awe (or Dread) of Isaac—making a sarcastic reference to God frightening Laban. Jacob finally has his going-away party, saying a prayer and sharing a meal.

In contrast to his greeting Jacob with a kiss when he arrived in Haran (29:13), Laban departs with no display of affection toward his son-in-law. He kisses his daughters and grandchildren good-bye, offers them his blessing, and goes home.

Jacob and Laban were doomed from the start. Con artists are not meant to live with other con artists. Neither of these two swindlers trusted the other, but they benefited from their relationship.

Grace that Overcomes Conflict and Makes Us Family

Good people who read Bible commentaries may have trouble with shifty characters like Jacob, but we should find hope in the way God cares for Jacob. Our place in God's family, like Jacob's, is a gift.

God gives immeasurable grace to con artists, deceitful sons-in-law, thieving daughters, sneaky painters, and Sunday school teachers. Recognizing God's astonishing mercy opens our hearts. We experience the grace of accepting others as family, even if they are dishonest with us, for through grace we know that they belong to the same hope to which we belong and are accepted with the same love with which we have been accepted.

Notes

Notes

4

RECONCILIATION

Genesis 32:3-32

Central Question

To what lengths will I go to be reconciled?

Scripture

Genesis 32:3-32 Jacob sent messengers before him to his brother Esau in the land of Seir, the country of Edom, 4 instructing them, "Thus you shall say to my lord Esau: Thus says your servant Jacob, 'I have lived with Laban as an alien, and stayed until now; 5 and I have oxen, donkeys, flocks, male and female slaves; and I have sent to tell my lord, in order that I may find favor in your sight.'" 6 The messengers returned to Jacob, saying, "We came to your brother Esau, and he is coming to meet you, and four hundred men are with him." 7 Then Jacob was greatly afraid and distressed; and he divided the people that were with him, and the flocks and herds and camels, into two companies, 8 thinking, "If Esau comes to the one company and destroys it, then the company that is left will escape." 9 And Jacob said, "O God of my father Abraham and God of my father Isaac, O LORD who said to me, 'Return to your country and to your kindred, and I will do you good,' 10 I am not worthy of the least of all the steadfast love and all the faithfulness that you have shown to your servant, for with only my staff I crossed this Jordan; and now I have become two companies. 11 Deliver me, please, from the hand of my brother, from the hand of Esau, for I am afraid of him; he may come and kill us all, the mothers with the children. 12 Yet you have said, 'I will surely do you good, and make your offspring as the sand of the sea, which cannot be counted because of their number.'" 13 So he spent that night there, and from what he had with him he took a present for his brother Esau, 14 two hundred female goats and twenty male goats, two hundred ewes and twenty rams, 15 thirty milch camels and their colts, forty cows and ten bulls, twenty female donkeys and ten male donkeys. 16 These he delivered into the hand of his servants, every drove by itself, and said to his servants, "Pass on ahead of me, and put a space between drove and drove." 17 He instructed the foremost, "When Esau my brother meets you, and asks you, 'To whom do you belong? Where are you going? And whose are these ahead of you?' 18 then you shall say, 'They belong to your servant Jacob; they are a present sent to my lord Esau; and moreover he is behind us.'" 19 He likewise instructed the second and the third and all who followed the droves, "You shall say the same thing to Esau when you meet him, 20 and you shall say, 'Moreover your servant Jacob is behind us.'" For he thought, "I may appease him with the present that goes ahead of me, and afterwards I shall see his face; perhaps he will accept me." 21 So the present passed on ahead of him; and he himself spent that night in the camp. 22 The same night he got up and took his two wives, his two maids, and his eleven children, and crossed the ford of the Jabbok. 23 He took them and sent them across the stream, and likewise everything that he had. 24 Jacob was left alone; and a man wrestled with him until daybreak. 25 When the man saw that he did not prevail against Jacob, he struck him on the hip socket; and Jacob's hip was put out of joint as he wrestled with him. 26 Then he said, "Let me go, for the day is breaking." But Jacob said, "I will not let you go, unless you bless me." 27 So he said to him, "What is your name?" And he said, "Jacob." 28 Then the man said, "You shall no longer be called Jacob, but Israel, for you have striven with God and with humans, and have prevailed." 29 Then Jacob asked him, "Please tell me your name." But he said, "Why is it that you ask my name?" And there he blessed him. 30 So Jacob called the place Peniel, saying, "For I have seen God face to face, and yet my life is preserved." 31 The sun rose upon him as he passed Peniel, limping because of his hip. 32 Therefore to this day the Israelites do not eat the thigh muscle that is on the hip socket, because he struck Jacob on the hip socket at the thigh muscle.

Reflecting

Susan sat in the car numbly, looking at the quiet suburban house that lay beyond. Yes, this was the address.

It had been twelve years since Susan had seen her parents. What would they look like? What would they say? Would they hug her? Would they slap her or call the police?

Caught up in a life of drugs and the clutches of an abusive boyfriend, Susan had run away from home at seventeen. She could hardly summarize the years that had followed. They had passed almost in a dream. She had suffered a miscarriage and then, remarkably, given birth to a healthy daughter. Motherhood briefly jolted her to sobriety, but soon her addictions took over again. She slipped back into old habits.

One night, sitting in a portable toilet where she had gone to throw up, she asked God to help her. Many addicts have prayed similar prayers under such circumstances, but for Susan, the simple heartfelt prayer seemed to take on a power of its own.

She entered rehab and then a twelve-step program at an inner-city church. She reclaimed her daughter and the two began attending worship. The warmth and love they experienced there gave Susan the stability she needed to heal and transform. Volunteers helped her get her GED and a job. Eventually, Susan got married. Her husband, a volunteer minister at the church, was loving and supportive.

But she still had deep wounds. She regretted so much. Most of all, she regretted the suffering she had caused her parents. Still, she had not been able to bring herself to contact them.

"Now or never," she muttered. She took a deep breath, walked to the door, and rang the bell.

Studying

Like Susan, Jacob was going home. Twenty years before, the brash, immature young man had schemed to cheat his brother, Esau, out of the blessing intended for the firstborn. In retaliation, his brother had plotted to kill him (Gen 27:41). Jacob was forced to flee, taking refuge with his mother's family in far-off Aram.

For Jacob, those years in exile were full of activity. He married twice and fathered eleven sons and a daughter. Though he had run away with only the clothes on his back, in exile he prospered. God blessed him. He became almost as successful as Abraham, his larger-than-life grandfather (32:5; see 24:35).

> After twenty years of separation, the reader recalls that the last words we heard from Esau were, "I will kill my brother Jacob" (27.41). Jacob's preparations to meet Esau exhibit great anxiety about whether Esau still carries this threat with him (v. 11). OT 45

Then God told Jacob it was time to go home. "Return to the land of your ancestors and to your kindred," God said, "and I will be with you" (31:3). The promise comforted Jacob. But what about Esau? Did his brother still hold a grudge? Did he still want to kill him?

Jacob takes no chances. He decides to address the situation directly and do all he can to make amends.

First, he gathers information. Where is Esau now? He finds his brother in Seir, southwest of the Dead Sea, where Esau's descendants would eventually settle. Through a messenger, Jacob makes contact.

Jacob lets Esau know that he has been living with their uncle in Aram and thus out of touch for many years. He also lets Esau know that he has become quite wealthy. This is not mere boasting. Jacob wants Esau to know that he no longer covets the family wealth that once divided them. Probably, Jacob is also hinting that he wants to do whatever he can financially to "make things right." Jacob even calls his brother "my lord" (32:4). For a man to address his brother in that way, he must truly be desperate! Jacob offers an olive branch, but will Esau take it?

The messengers return. They found Esau, and Esau is now on his way to meet Jacob. So far, so good.

Then they add, "and four hundred men are with him" (32:6). The words likely sent a chill up Jacob's spine. Four *hundred* men? An earlier story tells how Abraham had assembled 318 "trained men" from his household to rescue a nephew kidnapped by warlords (14:14). Likely the same family militia now accompanies Esau on the way to meet Jacob.

Jacob springs into fearful action. Strategically, he divides his caravan into two flanks, so that if Esau attacks, at least some of them can escape (32:7-8). Next, Jacob prays, reminding God of the promise to deliver him home safely and asking for protection from his brother (32:9-12). Finally, he prepares an unbelievably generous peace offering of livestock for his brother in the hope that it will assuage Esau's anger. The animals are artfully spaced out and presented so as to make the gift as impressive as possible (32:13-21) (Sarna, 225).

Jacob crosses the Jabbok River repeatedly in his preparations, laboring over every detail for the crucial meeting with Esau the next day. Finally, Jacob himself, for reasons that are unclear, chooses to remain alone on the other side. There, the Scripture says, "a man wrestled with him until daybreak" (32:24).

The Jabbok was a fast-flowing tributary of the Jordan River just north of the Dead Sea, identified with the Zarqa River of modern-day Jordan. Probably Jacob and his family crossed on stepping stones and timber that were placed in some of the river's shallowest waters. It must have been extremely dangerous for a large caravan to cross by night under such circumstances; that he made the crossing further indicates Jacob's desperation (Sarna, 226–27; Younker, 3:593–94).

Who is this mysterious stranger? What does he want? Generations later, Jacob's descendants identify him as an angel (Hos 3:4). At the time, Jacob only knows that he is in the fight of his life. Neither opponent can prevail. Eventually, the stranger manages to wrench Jacob's hip out of socket. Still, the tenacious Jacob refuses to yield.

"Let me go, for day is breaking," says the stranger. Perhaps this made Jacob question the stranger's character. Was he a river

god, some kind of demon, or another spirit?

Jacob, perhaps awakening to the possibility that he was no longer "wrestling with flesh and blood," refuses to release the stranger without a blessing. The stranger asks Jacob's name, and he gives it. In Hebrew, Jacob (*ya'aqob*) means "deceiver" or "supplanter." It has been both his name and his character throughout life. The stranger tells him he now has a new name. He will be called Israel (*yisra'el*), one who has struggled with God and overcome.

Gustave Doré, *Jacob Wrestling with the Angel*

Understanding

After all the haste to get his family across the river, why did Jacob choose to remain alone on the other side? The campsite was full of noisy, anxious people. Perhaps Jacob simply wanted peace and quiet.

However, he did not find peace on either side of the river. Jacob could not find peace until Jacob himself was at peace. Jacob's mind swirled with fears, doubts, and his own plans. He suffered from painful experiences with his father's family long ago and with his mother's family more recently. For all his machinations, peace was not something Jacob could force or create. For Jacob to experience peace, he first, through the grace of God, had to be at peace within himself.

Many of us are like this. We think peace is something that happens *to* us. We think that if we can only get others to behave in a certain way, we will have peace. This is an illusion. As long as we are not at peace within, there is nowhere we can run, no direction where we can turn, to find it. Peace does not exist on either side of the river. This is why God confronted Jacob. Jacob's true conflict was spiritual. The challenge was not to arrange the people and livestock in the most appealing way. The challenge was for Jacob to shed his old nature and become new.

God fought with Jacob so Jacob would take away the blessing he truly needed: not the blessing of his father, but the blessing of God, the capacity for transformation. With that blessing in hand, finally at peace within, Jacob was now ready to seek peace outside himself as well.

What About Me?

• *The unresolved wounds and conflicts of the past create future difficulties for us or our descendants.* What conflicts, open or beneath the surface, exist in your relationships with family members, friends, or in your workplace or church family?

• *We must take concrete actions to make peace possible. Jacob gathered information.* He sent messengers to contact his brother and arrange for a meeting. He prepared a gift to make amends for the pain he had caused. What steps could you take to be reconciled with someone?

• *Before we can experience peace in our relationships, we must be at peace within ourselves.* If we are full of anger, fear, anxiety, and conflict, then we are unable to live at peace with others. When do you nurture solitude and silence? When you are alone and still, what thoughts and images course through your mind? What steps could you take to be more at peace within?

• *Peace is a spiritual matter.* True peace comes from our encounter with the divine. What is the nature of your relationship with God? How is God pushing you to shed old patterns of thinking and living and become new? If your name were based on your inner character at its most basic level, what would that name be? If you, like Jacob, wrestled with God, what name and character do you think God would give you?

Resources

Walter Brueggemann, *Genesis* (Atlanta: John Knox, 1982).

Nahum M. Sarna, *Genesis* (Philadelphia: Jewish Publication Society, 1989).

Gordan J. Wenham, *Genesis 16–50* (Dallas: Word, 1994).

Randall W. Younker, "Jabbok," *The Anchor Bible Dictionary* (New York: Doubleday, 1992).

RECONCILIATION

Genesis 32:3-32

Fear that Leads to Faith

Some might think that if we believe what others teach us about God, then God will make our lives easy, good people will always live comfortably, and God will keep us from all trouble. As many believers can attest, it does not work that way. God does not form us into God's people through a trouble-free existence. God makes us who we are meant to be through struggles and hardships. We end up frightened at times, wrestling with a God who will not let us go.

On the bank of the Jabbok River, Jacob wrestles with becoming a better person. Jacob started wrestling before he was born. When they entered the world, Jacob was trying to break his brother's ankle. They kept wrestling. Jacob tricked Esau into trading his birthright for a bowl of chili. While their father presumably lay dying, Jacob fooled the old man into giving him, not Esau, the family inheritance. Esau said he would kill his brother for it, so Jacob went on the run. He worked for Laban for twenty years in exchange for two daughters and everything he could sneak away.

Now he is finally, fearfully, coming home. Jacob's dread at meeting Esau is hardly surprising in light of the way he has treated his big brother. They will soon stand face to face. Will Esau forgive him or kill him? Jacob has every reason to assume Esau is out for blood.

Jacob is Terrified (32:3-12)

It seems that Jacob heads toward his old home in Beer-sheba (28:10) by a route to the east and south of the Dead Sea that approaches Esau's home in Edom (33:12-14). Jacob takes elaborate precautions to try to calm Esau. Ever the wheeler-dealer, Jacob offers livestock as a gift or a bribe—whichever is more acceptable. He sends representatives with these instructions: "When you see Esau, say, 'Your servant Jacob has been stuck with Laban for a long time. He now has all kinds of flocks and slaves that he would be happy to share.'"

Jacob "lays it on with a trowel," stressing the repeated phrases "my lord" and "your servant," but the first exchange between Jacob and Esau is ominous (Henry Wansbrough, *Genesis* [New York: Doubleday, 1998] 77). All diplomacy seems brushed aside. The succinct response from Jacob's envoys that Esau is on his way with 400 men scares Jacob into thinking that the cavalry is coming for him.

Jacob falls apart. He divides his people and property into two companies. His idea is that if Esau attacks one half, the other half can get away.

Jacob starts praying. "God of my father and grandfather, you told me to go home, and that is what I am trying to do. You said you would treat me well. I know I don't deserve the goodness you have sent my way. I only had the shirt on my back when I left home, and now two huge camps travel with me. Save me from Esau. He could kill all of us. You promised to do good for me. I am supposed to have countless descendants."

Jacob Comes Up with an Elaborate Strategy (32:13-21)

Jacob puts together quite a gift to mollify Esau—220 goats, 220 sheep, 30 milk camels, 40 cows, 10 bulls, and 30 donkeys. He instructs his servants to march in groups like bands in a parade.

When Esau approaches the first group and asks who they are, they are to say, "We belong to your servant Jacob, but now we belong to you. He is right behind us." (In fact, Jacob plans to be way behind them. If he hears screams, he will rethink the idea of a family reunion.)

How can all of these gifts not soften Esau? Jacob figures it is hard to attack someone who just paid for your children's college education.

Some scholars suggest that we read two alternative traditions in Genesis. It is odd that there is no reference to the elaborate gifts later when the two men actually meet.

At this point, Jacob tells his family that he will spend the night by himself, but he does not tell them why he wants to be alone. He may not know why.

God Shows Up (32:22-32)

Jacob sends everyone across the river and spends the night far behind the parade of payoffs. The Jabbok flows into the Jordan just below the Lake of Galilee, forming a break in the eastern hills from which Jacob comes after leaving Laban. It is puzzling that Jacob should attempt to cross the river (let alone at night with his people and his flocks). The river does not seem to lie on his route, and the next time we see Jacob he is, as before, on the north side of it (Wansbrough, 78).

In the middle of the night, out of the darkness, a stranger jumps on Jacob and rolls him over. They wrestle shoulder to jaw, elbow to throat, knee to the back. This is big-time wrestling.

The stranger wants Jacob's life. It is terrible for Jacob not to know the one with whom he fights. Everything is shadows. Is it Esau meeting him early? Is it a night spirit, a ghost prowling in the darkness? Is it a river sprite believed to keep travelers from crossing rivers? Is it a demon that lives there in the middle of nowhere? Is Jacob wrestling with himself, struggling with his own demons? Is it an angel? Is it the God who has haunted him all his life?

They struggle until just before morning, when it looks for a moment as though Jacob will win. Then suddenly, everything is reversed when the stranger knocks Jacob's hip out of joint and says, "I quit. We have wrestled all night."

Jacob is crippled, defeated, and helpless, but he clings for dear life, holding on like a drowning man. "Nobody quits until you give me your blessing."

Gasping for breath, the stranger asks, "What is your name?"

"It's Jacob."

The stranger says, "It's not Jacob anymore. It's Israel—God perseveres. You have wrestled with God and people, and you have not been defeated."

The gift of a name represents not only a new status, but also a sense of possession by one who gives the name. The name "Jacob" means "to deceive." His new name, "Israel," could be translated "the one God rules."

Jacob asks for the stranger's name, but the stranger refuses to give Jacob any power over him and offers a blessing instead.

The darkness fades enough for Jacob to see his opponent's face dimly. This is not the gracious God of the daylight, always gentle and comforting. This is the terrifying force of the God of night, a God who wants nothing to do with an easy faith.

The story wavers over the identity of the opponent, initially calling him a "man" but finally granting that Jacob has "seen God face to face." Jacob names the place Peniel ("God's face"), saying, "I saw God and am still around to tell about it."

The site of Penuel (which is called "Peniel" only in v. 30) is said to be the eastern one of two mounds where the Jabbok enters the Jordan Valley. A town was later built there (Jdg 8:8; 1 Kgs 12:25).

This experience at Penuel is Jacob's second critical encounter with God (see 28:10-22). The God who promised to bring Jacob back to the land of Canaan (28:15) encounters him in deathly struggle on this return, changes his name, and cripples him before blessing him. Struggle is a dominant theme in Jacob's story.

The account ends with a brief aside, Jacob "limping because of his hip." The Jewish custom referenced here of not eating the sinew of the hip socket is not mentioned anywhere else in the Bible (32:32).

Are we stretching to think of Jacob's limp as a gift? The con artist cannot run anymore. Jacob is wounded as God takes final possession of him. This mysterious encounter makes an honest person out of him. Jacob's experience with the divine prepares him for the challenge of being reconciled with his brother. Jacob has been reborn as Israel, the one who has faced God, been gripped by God, and struggled with God.

Wrestling with God

Wrestling with God is dangerous business. Nobody wants to end up limping, so we are tempted to accept an easy faith that avoids struggles and never tackles hard questions. We want to believe that God makes no demands.

However, we are not formed by success and a trouble-free existence. We are molded by our struggles. Sooner or later, every one of us wrestles with the Eternal Stranger who will not let us go. We wind up feeling alone in some God-forsaken wilderness with danger all around, when the things we thought would hold forever fall apart. We never know when things will take a turn and we will suddenly find ourselves face to face with our deepest fears. At such moments, we need to know how to struggle until morning, how to hold on to grace (Bill Leonard, Baccalaureate Address, Wake Forest University, 16 May 1999).

We are tempted to avoid any danger that might leave a scar and to keep our distance from any flame that might burn us. Country musician Garth Brooks wrote, "Life is not tried; it is merely survived if you're standing outside the fire."

Some people never learn to struggle with faith. Hard questions simply do not trouble them. Hardships never make them wonder about what they have always believed.

But for most of us, life is hard. Tragedies strike—a sister is gone, a husband, a friend. Children are born with terrible problems. Cancer, divorces, and business reversals make us wonder who is in charge and why the world does not work the way it ought to.

We have moments when we realize that we are not as certain as we once were. It is not clear what God is doing, what God is trying to say to us, or what God wants from us. The easy answers do not work. What does it mean to say that God is almighty when we pray for someone we love to be healed and they die anyway? Why could Jesus feed five thousand with five loaves and two fish when thousands of children now starve every day? Why is life so hard?

God engages us in the struggle of life because God wants to make us new people. The Bible pictures God as a potter who pounds, pushes, molds, hammers, and whirls a hunk of clay on a wheel until he forms a pot that can offer someone a cup of cold water in God's name (Elizabeth Achtemeier, *Pulpit Resource* [4 August 1996] 21). Some of our encounters with God are not sweet, amazing grace so much as they are tough, assaulting grace.

Could it be that before we can truly love God, we have to wrestle with God? God struggles with us to rule our lives, to pull us into the good purposes that God is working out. It is not always a pleasant experience. God may grab, fight, and jerk us around to walk a new path that we had not dreamed of taking. It costs us to wrestle with God, to have God push at us until we reflect God's hopes.

If we want to live deeply, then we may end up limping, but the people who know the blessing of God are the ones who struggle with God. Sometimes our encounters with God are painful, but through the pain we become God's people.

Notes

Notes

5

CLOSURE

Genesis 33:1-17; 35:27-29

Central Question

What past fears and conflicts do I need to put behind me?

Scripture

Genesis 33:1-17; 35:27-29 Now Jacob looked up and saw Esau coming, and four hundred men with him. So he divided the children among Leah and Rachel and the two maids. 2 He put the maids with their children in front, then Leah with her children, and Rachel and Joseph last of all. 3 He himself went on ahead of them, bowing himself to the ground seven times, until he came near his brother. 4 But Esau ran to meet him, and embraced him, and fell on his neck and kissed him, and they wept. 5 When Esau looked up and saw the women and children, he said, "Who are these with you?" Jacob said, "The children whom God has graciously given your servant." 6 Then the maids drew near, they and their children, and bowed down; 7 Leah likewise and her children drew near and bowed down; and finally Joseph and Rachel drew near, and they bowed down. 8 Esau said, "What do you mean by all this company that I met?" Jacob answered, "To find favor with my lord." 9 But Esau said, "I have enough, my brother; keep what you have for yourself." 10 Jacob said, "No, please; if I find favor with you, then accept my present from my hand; for truly to see your face is like seeing the face of God—since you have received me with such favor. 11 Please accept my gift that is brought to you, because God has dealt graciously with me, and because I have everything I want." So he urged him, and he took it. 12 Then Esau said, "Let us journey on our way, and I will go alongside you." 13 But Jacob said to him, "My lord knows that the children are frail and that the flocks and herds, which are nursing, are a care to me; and if they are overdriven for one day, all the flocks will die. 14 Let my lord pass on ahead of his servant, and I will lead on slowly, according to the pace of the cattle that are before me and according to the pace of the children, until I come to my lord in Seir." 15 So Esau said, "Let me leave with you some of the people who are with me." But he said, "Why should my lord be so kind to me?" 16 So Esau returned that day on his way to Seir. 17 But Jacob journeyed to Succoth, and built himself a house, and made booths for his cattle; therefore the place is called Succoth.... 35:27 Jacob came to his father Isaac at Mamre, or Kiriath-arba (that is, Hebron), where Abraham and Isaac had resided as aliens. 28 Now the days of Isaac were one hundred eighty years. 29 And Isaac breathed his last; he died and was gathered to his people, old and full of days; and his sons Esau and Jacob buried him.

Reflecting

"No," he screamed, "this can't be happening! My father! My father!" The words came from a handsome man in his fifties kneeling at a hospital bed. In the bed lay an unconscious man in his eighties. The elderly man had suffered a stroke and was unlikely to live long. The doctors recommended that he be made a DNR: "do not resuscitate."

Most of the family seemed willing to accept this. They did not want their father to suffer. He would not want to be "hooked up to machines," they said.

But the fifty-year-old son resisted. A nurse arrived and gently touched the weeping man on the shoulder, and the family's story began to unfold. When the younger man was two, his father had abandoned him and moved to a distant state, remarrying and raising two daughters. His new family always thought of him as a good and loving father. He never told them about the son from his past.

The son grew into adulthood. He grew curious about his father and hired an investigator to find him. He contacted his father by phone, and his father seemed eager to meet him. But on the day of their planned reunion, his father suddenly suffered from a stroke.

? How can we put painful memories and unresolved feelings behind us? Do we ever *really* get over the hurts and regrets of the past?

In time, the son was able to let his father go. That night he spent an hour at the bedside of his unconscious father, pouring out his heart. After the funeral, he wrote him a series of letters. The son also developed a relationship with his two half-sisters. The women told him stories about his father. In time, with the support of family, friends, and a skilled counselor, the son was able to be at peace with the father he had never known.

Studying

Our final session deals with Jacob's long-awaited encounter with Esau. The passage immediately follows the events of last session. After twenty years of exile, Jacob returns home. He has sent word to Esau, along with indications that he wants to make amends. Hearing that Esau is on the way with 400 men, Jacob panics, hastily preparing a lavish gift to appease his brother—and taking defensive measures to protect himself should that fail. Meanwhile, Jacob engages in a nighttime struggle with a mysterious stranger who blesses him and gives him a new name.

The fight is now over, and the sun is rising (32:31). Jacob sees Esau and his men (33:1). Jacob, who has already tediously arranged everything, continues to line everyone up (with Rachel and Joseph, his favorites, in the back—the safest position of all). Jacob himself now surges past everyone to the front of the line.

An observer watching from a distant peak would have seen a bewildering spectacle. On one side marches a veritable army. On the other comes a sprawling caravan of sheep, goats, camels, and other livestock, plus adults and children of every age, as if arranged for a parade down Main Street. A man with a distinct limp weaves his way through them all (31:31). Advancing to meet the other group, he throws himself onto the ground again and again—seven times in all.

Clearly, Jacob is penitent, but can there ever be peace between these two men? Verse 4 gives the answer: "But Esau ran to meet him, and embraced him, and fell on his neck and kissed him, and they wept." Yes, peace is possible, even for Jacob and Esau!

Esau then asks about the women and children, and Jacob makes introductions. For the first time, Esau meets his nephews, nieces, and sisters-in-law.

Then there is the "gift." Jacob has set aside a considerable portion of livestock—550 animals in all—as a peace offering for his brother (32:15-16). Jacob knows he has caused his brother considerable pain. While no financial blessing can fully repay the damage, he wants to do what he can. At first, following the etiquette of the time (Sarna, 230), Esau refuses: "I have enough, my brother; keep what you have for yourself" (33:9).

Jacob, however, insists, and the language of his reply gives two important clues to his intent. First, he says that to see his brother's face is "like seeing the face of God" (33:10). Jacob has just survived a face-to-face encounter with God and named the place Peniel, "Face of God" (32:30). He has struggled with God and "prevailed" (32:28). However, he prevailed not by *winning*—the fight was a stalemate—but through suffering and perseverance. It is also that way regarding Esau. Ultimately, as is often the case in conflicts, neither party is able to "win." But through suffering, perseverance, and commitment to the relationship, peace is possible. Esau's smiling face, his willingness to accept his brother, mirrors the grace Jacob received from God the night before.

> Bowing seven times was the gesture of a subject before his or her king, or of a slave before his or her master.

Second, in the Hebrew of verse 11, Jacob refers to the "present" as a "blessing" (translated by the NRSV simply as "gift"). The significance of that word was not likely lost on Esau, whom Jacob had cheated out of blessing years before. At least symbolically, Jacob tries to give the blessing back. This is probably also the significance of "bowing down" to Esau (33:6; see 27:29)

(Sarna, 229–30; Wenham, 298–99). This is no idle apology. Jacob does everything possible to put things right.

At Jacob's insistence, Esau accepts the offering. Then, presuming that Jacob has set out to meet him in Seir, Esau offers to accompany his brother on the journey. Jacob, whether out of lingering doubts about their relationship or for other reasons, politely turns down Esau's offer to serve as bodyguard (Wenham, 300). But in time, he insists, they will meet again (33:14).

They do in fact meet again, at least once more. The final scene involves the death of their father, Isaac. Isaac had summoned Esau to receive the family blessing long before, thinking he was unlikely to live long (27:2). In fact, he lived twenty more years! Ironically, while fear of death drove the brothers apart, death itself brings them together. Together, the brothers lay their father to rest (35:29; cf. 25:9).

Understanding

The story of Jacob and Esau is one of lifelong conflict. Pitted against one another by parents, the customs of society, and their own weaknesses and ambitions, the two led their whole lives in opposition.

How would it end? Like Cain and Abel, would one finally kill the other? Jacob took the first step toward reconciliation. Rather than vengeance, Esau too desired a fresh start with his brother. He ran to meet him, hugged and kissed him, and wept (33:4). The story ends with both brothers united at their father's funeral.

Jesus told a beautiful story that echoes this one, which we know as the parable of the Prodigal Son (Luke 15:11-32). It too is about a farm family, a father and two sons. Somewhat like Jacob, the younger son secured a portion of the estate from his father and quickly ran off to a distant pagan land.

At this point, the stories diverge. While Jacob married, had children, and achieved

> The last days of Isaac provide an occasion for reconciliation between Jacob and his father (v. 27; see 27.35). The two sons, Esau and Jacob, join together in burying their father, Isaac (v. 29), just as earlier the brothers Isaac and Ishmael had joined together to bury their father, Abraham (25.9).

financial success, the man in Jesus' story squandered every dime in bohemian decadence. In time, however, he came to his senses and returned home. While he was still on the way, the *father* ran out to meet him, welcoming him with hugs and kisses.

"But wait," Jesus' listeners might have asked, "isn't it the *older brother* who is supposed to meet the younger and receive him with kisses? Where is the older brother?" In Jesus' story, the older brother sulks in the distance, out of relationship with his father and brother (Lk 15:28).

Only in comparison with the story of Jacob and Esau does the story of the Prodigal Son take on its full meaning. Listening to Jesus, we are compelled to ask, "If Esau could forgive his brother, why can't we?"

What About Me?

• *Peace is not a matter of winning and losing.* As long as we view a relationship as a win-lose contest, we cannot be at peace. Think of a conflict in which you are or have been involved. Do (did) you identify your struggle in terms of winning and losing? In what other ways could you view it?

• *Someone must take the first step in reconciliation.* Often, each party in a conflict waits, hoping the other will flinch first. Neither wants to appear "weak." If this happens, the conflict will continue indefinitely. Think of a conflict. What steps could you take to put an end to it? In what ways could these efforts backfire, fail, or be misinterpreted? Are those risks worth the chance of redeeming the relationship?

• *We can't outrun our conflicts.* Jacob could not outrun his conflict with Esau. Though he traveled a great distance, he simply found the conflict repeated in his relationship with Laban. After all, the conflict was within Jacob. Likewise, if we cut off one relationship of conflict, we often find ourselves facing the same conflict in a new form. We may find a new spouse, a new job, or a new church, but the conflict remains. It becomes part of our relational nature.

How can we face our conflicts and find resolution, both within ourselves and with others?

• *Resolving differences requires honesty and compassion.* Jacob and Esau were finally able to resolve their differences. With God's help, we too can find peace. Even if face-to-face resolution is not possible, we can still find peace. Just as it is possible to carry conflict with us into new relationships, it is possible to carry reconciliation and peace with us too. Consider the story in the "Reflecting" section. How else might a person find inner reconciliation with a loved one who has died?

Resource

Walter Brueggemann, *Genesis* (Atlanta: John Knox, 1982).

Edwin H. Friedman, *Generation to Generation* (New York: Guilford, 1985).

Nahum M. Sarna, *Genesis* (Philadelphia: Jewish Publication Society, 1989).

Gordan J. Wenham, *Genesis 16–50* (Dallas: Word, 1994).

CLOSURE

Genesis 33:1-17; 35:27-29

Covering Up

"You should wear a hat."

In twenty-six years, this was the first time I remember Carol saying, "You should wear a hat."

I responded appropriately. "Huh?"

"Like when you were in college. You wore hats then. Maybe you should get a fedora."

Carol and I did not meet until after college, but I let it pass. Several days later, I realized what was going on. My beloved thinks it is time for me to start covering my bald spot. "Spot" may not be the right word. Spot sounds like a speck or a dot. My bald area is yarmulke-sized and threatening to become a bald head rather than a bald spot. My sweetie thinks it is time to take cover, so I am shopping for a fedora.

We want to keep our bald spots as well as other embarrassments out of sight. Most of us know the feeling of wanting to cover our heads or being in way over our heads. This sense of inadequacy is usually accompanied by concern over whether we can keep it hidden. We hope to slide by without anyone realizing that we are not who we hope we appear to be.

We are mixed bags of virtue and vice, humility and arrogance, love and apathy. We try to keep our vice, arrogance, and apathy under wraps. Most people pretend, avoid, and evade.

How humiliating would it be if everyone knew our exact thoughts all the time? How quickly would our friends realize that they do not know us as well as they think they do?

We hope no one finds out how imperfect we are. We worry not only about the bad things we have done, but about who we are.

We are troubled not only by our mistakes, but also by the short-comings that led to those mistakes. Our negative feelings about ourselves are more pervasive than our guilt about what we have done. We need forgiveness not merely for what we do, but also for who we are. We want to conceal what is deep inside—even from God.

Jake the Snake and His Gracious Brother (33:1-7)

The Bible is filled with frauds who are not the people they appear to be and hope that no one realizes their true identities—especially not God. The writers tell their stories with remarkable honesty. Jacob is one of the heroes of the Jewish people, and yet no effort is made to gloss over his faults. Genesis makes no attempt to obscure the fact that Jacob is, among other things, a crook. What is more, it seems that whoever wrote about his seamy adventures got a kick out of them. Jacob keeps getting into situations he must get out of quickly.

God continues to forgive Jacob, even though God knows better than anyone that the man is a thief and a liar. God's forgiveness doesn't change Jacob as much as it would if we were writing the story. Surprisingly, Jacob remains a scoundrel.

At the beginning of Genesis 33, it seems like Jacob's past may catch up with him. Esau earlier vowed to kill his brother (27:41). Jacob may finally get what is due him.

Jacob gulps when he sees Esau approaching with 400 men. An army of that size seems like enough to make one hesitate. Jacob arranges his family into a parade. He puts the least precious of his wives (and their children) nearest the possibly hostile troops and keeps his beloved Rachel (and her son) at the back, farthest from danger.

Jacob is still manipulative and deceitful, but at least he takes his chances in front of the crowd rather than at the back. His midnight wrestling match (32:24-32) may have something to do with his choice to lead the procession. Jacob, now also known as "Israel," seeks reconciliation, walking with humility as well as a limp after his struggle with God.

Jacob greets Esau with oriental formality, showing great respect by bowing seven times to the ground. Esau will have nothing of it. The rough-and-tumble outdoorsman responds to the elaborate ceremonial bows with the heartiest and least formal of hugs. He kisses Jacob. Rather than vengeance, Esau wants a fresh start with his brother.

He points to the procession and asks, "Who is this?"

Jacob answers, "These are children God gave me, your servant."

In what is surely quite a spectacle, each company marches up to Esau and bows—maidservants, Leah's brood, Rachel and Joseph.

Jacob insists on calling his brother "my lord." He assumes that if Esau accepts the gifts, then he will be obligated to let Jacob be, but if Esau refuses the gifts, he is free to do his brother harm. Jacob is still not sure how this will end. "I was hoping that you would see these gifts as a gesture of good will," he says. He has worked on his speech like a lawyer pleading for mercy. "Whatever I have is yours."

Esau echoes a little of the devil-may-care attitude he had about his birthright decades earlier—"of what use is a birthright to me?" (25:33)—when he says, "I have enough" (33:9).

Jacob Has Trouble Believing Esau's Forgiveness (33:10-17)

Jacob begs, "Accept these gifts in the hope that we can be better brothers than we have been. When I saw your face, it looked like the face of God smiling at me." The reference to "seeing the face of God" ties this story to Jacob's experience on the bank of the Jabbok River (32:30).

The encounter with God and the renewal of family ties are not the same, but they cannot be completely separated. In the holy God, there is something of the estranged brother. In the forgiving brother, there is something of the blessing God. Jacob has seen the face of God. Now he knows that seeing the face of Esau is like that. The forgiving face of Esau and the blessing face of God have an affinity (Walter Brueggemann, *Genesis* [Atlanta: John Knox, 1986] 272–73).

Jacob continues, "Please take the gifts. I won't miss them. Call it a peace offering."

After observing the proprieties of polite refusal, Esau accepts Jacob's extravagant gifts. This may restore the material equilibrium between them that was disturbed by the loss both of Esau's birthright (25:19-34) and his paternal blessing from Isaac (27:1-41).

Esau says, "Let's get a move on. I'll lead the way."

Jacob replies, "You can see that we are moving pretty slow. The children are not doing well. Some of the sheep and cattle are newborn. If we try to stay with you, some of them won't make it. You go ahead and we'll follow at our leisurely pace."

Esau helpfully offers, "Let me lend you a few servants."

Jacob responds, "That's not necessary. Your kindness today is more than I could have imagined."

The cautious and calculating Jacob is determined not to prolong their meeting. He hustles Esau ahead with the excuse that his party cannot keep up.

Esau moves on to Seir, a mountainous desert in Edomite territory, and disappears for a time from the story. Jacob goes only a few miles to Succoth, a town on the east side of the Jordan Valley. One interpretation is that Jacob sent Esau ahead and then did not follow.

Isaac's Sons Bury Him—and the Hatchet (35:27-29)

Jacob and Esau do not meet again until they come together to bury their father. When the brothers separated (33:16-17), it seemed in some ways that they merely made a truce. These verses make it clear that they truly reconciled. The venom is removed from the oracle (25:23).

According to the chronology in Genesis 25:26 and 26:34, Isaac was 100 years old when Jacob left home. Given Isaac's condition at that time, it is surprising that he survived eighty more years (27:41). When Jacob finally makes it back home to Hebron, which had been Abraham's home and where Jacob will also be buried (50:12-14), Isaac is 180. Isaac dies after a full life. Esau and Jacob bury their father just as Isaac and Ishmael buried Abraham (25:9). The brothers' shared story ends at their father's funeral.

The Forgiving Face of God

When Jacob met Esau after all those years apart, he was surprised that Esau had forgiven him. Jacob saw God smiling in Esau's toothy grin. Jacob learned the wonderful lesson that thieves can steal many things, but they cannot steal acceptance of who they are. They, like anyone, can only receive it as a gift. Jacob learns that not only are there no crimes past forgiveness, there is also no part of us that is beyond forgiving.

We may mistakenly think of grace as something that shows up intermittently. We do something wrong, ask forgiveness, and God forgives us until we do something else wrong. The problem is that we keep doing wrong because that is part of who we are. Grace is bigger than forgiveness for each mistake. God's grace covers not only what we do, but who we are.

Salvation is accepting the acceptance of God, as Paul Tillich argued, and becoming more of who we already are, as Thomas Merton pointed out. God loves us in our limping and blessing, our bowing down and our forgiving.

Surprising Members of God's Family

Years ago, I was the pastor at youth camp. At about 1:00 a.m. on the first night, I heard a ruckus in the hall. I climbed out of bed to do my imitation of an assistant principal. I opened my door, shouted, "Hey," and gave them a minute to run back into their rooms. The boys scattered, except for one who got locked out.

Paul was a high school junior. He was not from my church, but he came to camp with us. He stood there in the hall, locked out of his room, completely naked. I received a fine theological education, but I do not recall being told how to respond to this particular situation.

"Paul, you are standing in the hall at 1:00 a.m. completely naked. Can you explain that?"

Paul says, "I was sleepwalking."

"Paul, I'm pretty sleepy, but I do not believe that."

"I didn't think you would, sir."

"Paul, why don't you knock on your door, put on some pajamas, and go to sleep?"

"Yes, sir."

I assumed that was the end of it, but it wasn't. The next morning, teenagers rushed to tell me that there was a rumor that I "caught a streaker outside at 3 a.m. and called the cops and who was it?"

I saw Paul, completely clothed this time, and suggested that he not mention our encounter to anyone else.

Eddie Haskell grinned and said, "I wish you had told me that earlier. I just got interviewed by the camp newspaper."

The next day, the front-page story was a lengthy exposé on Paul's adventure. When I got up to preach that night, no youth thought, "I must listen carefully for the word of God." They thought, "There's the old guy who caught the naked kid."

I was pleased not to have any contact with Paul for eleven years. Then one morning while in a meeting, I was handed a note that said Paul—"the sleepwalker from youth camp"—came by to say "Hi." He left a phone number. Paul is married, a seminary graduate, and a youth pastor at a Disciples of Christ church. By all accounts, he is a fine minister.

If you had asked me years ago to name the youth least likely to become a minister, I would have picked Paul, but I was wrong. Time passes. People change. God changes people because God stays with us.

Jacob seemed like the least likely person to do anything good, but Jacob of all people became not only the father of the twelve tribes of Israel, but the many times great-grandfather of Jesus.

God does not give us what we deserve. God gives us the grace that makes us family. God loves us not in spite of what we do, but because of who we are—God's beloved children.

Notes

Notes

www.ingramcontent.com/pod-product-compliance
Lightning Source LLC
Chambersburg PA
CBHW070552030426
42337CB00016B/2455